BOOKER T

FROM PRISON TO PROMISE

BOOKER T
FROM PRISON TO PROMISE

BOOKER T. HUFFMAN
WITH ANDREW WILLIAM WRIGHT

MEDALLION
P R E S S

Medallion Press, Inc.

Printed in USA

Published 2012 by Medallion Press, Inc.

The MEDALLION PRESS LOGO
is a registered trademark of Medallion Press, Inc.

Cover design by Adam Mock
Art direction by James Tampa
Edited by Emily Steele
Cover photography by Cody Bess www.codybess.com
Mug shot photo compliments of the Harris County Sheriff's Office.

Typeset in Adobe Garamond Pro
Printed in the United States of America

Cataloging-in-Publication Data is on file with the Library of Congress.

ISBN 978-1605424-68-2

10 9 8 7 6 5 4 3 2 1
First Edition

To my parents, Booker T Sr. and Rosa Huffman, may they forever rest in peace; my sister Carolyn Jones; and my wife, Sharmell, and our beautiful twin babies, Kendrick James and Kennedy Rose Huffman.

CONTENTS

sides, they were big and broad, loud, and in your face. While Booker and Lash portrayed menacing thugs who would send most people running for their lives, what stole the show was Booker's in-ring finesse. Booker combined long, sweeping karate kicks with agility and speed you would expect to see in a graceful ballet at Manhattan's Lincoln Center.

It was no surprise when Booker gradually separated from Lash and launched into a singles career, ensuring his rise to international stardom in both WCW and the WWF, now WWE (World Wrestling Entertainment). He won virtually every championship the organizations offered, including six individual world championships.

However, the history of Booker's meteoric rise in sports entertainment is a mere supplement to the story of his origins from the unforgiving streets of Houston. The following narrative documents Booker's remarkable and turbulent life from early childhood until the beginning of a career in WCW in his early adulthood. It chronicles a young man's tragic loss and struggle to survive, his troubled choices and their consequences, and the proverbial light at the end of the very dark tunnel his life became. *Booker T: From Prison to Promise* is a true story of calamity and redemption, and it is one you will never forget.

—Andrew William Wright

INTRODUCTION

Like most, I first encountered Booker T. Huffman on *World Championship Wrestling* (WCW) one night while randomly flipping through channels. It was mid-1996, and the professional wrestling industry had started to regain momentum after a relatively dormant period following the boom of the eighties. The product was experiencing a unique metamorphosis and had sharpened its image with a razor blade edge. Gone were the cartoonish and overly kid-friendly characters made famous in the World Wrestling Federation (WWF), such as Tito Santana, Koko B. Ware, and The Bushwhackers.

Now there were gritty, seemingly dangerous performers like the beer-pounding "Stone Cold" Steve Austin, Big Van Vader, and Sycho Sid Vicious, each who could and sometimes did leave an opponent legitimately injured in the ring. Even the heroic "say your prayers and take your vitamins" Hulk Hogan redefined himself as the black-clad, sinister Hollywood Hulk Hogan. Both WCW and WWF clashed every Monday night on cable TV and dominated the ratings with a newfound older audience of teens and twentysomethings. Professional wrestling was once again a hot commodity, and Booker T was right in the middle of the surge to the top.

Booker and his real-life brother Lash, known as Stevie Ray, performed as the tough-as-nails street-based tag team Harlem Heat. Wearing bright-red vinyl outfits with flames sewn up the

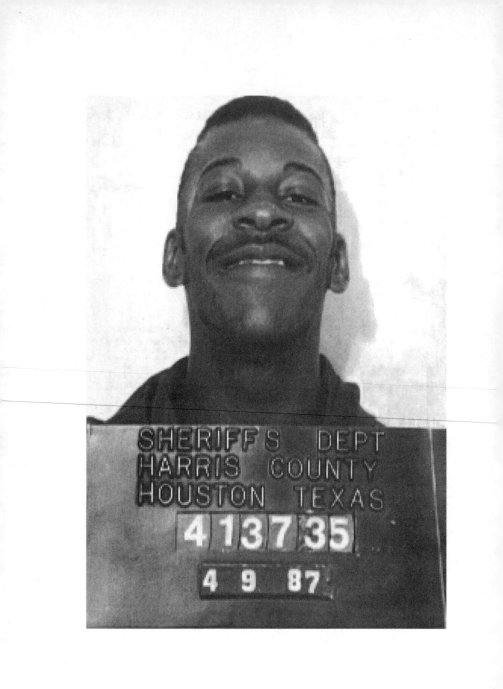

1

FROM THE STREETS TO THE SYSTEM

"Freeze! Hold it right there. Hands over your head."

I stood petrified, only one thought crashing through my mind. *Now what?*

A nightmare was unfolding before my very eyes. I couldn't grasp that it was actually happening, but it was—and mere feet from my front door. I could not concentrate on anything other than those drawn guns.

Two officers threw me to the ground. A knee smashed into my back, and my wrists were slapped into cuffs. One policeman underhooked my arms and picked me up while reading me my rights.

Defiantly, I did what I had been taught since childhood: I played ignorant. "Hey, man, what's goin' on? What's all this about?"

The one thing flashing through my brain was the advice of my sister Billie Jean, a streetwise hustler as cool as they came: *Junior, once you tell a lie, you've always got to stick to that first lie.* Even in the back of the cop car, I insisted, "I have no idea what you're talking about. You've got the wrong guy."

I was convinced no one could identify me. I was wrong. When they put me in a lineup at the station, I was instantly picked out.

Well, so much for ignorance. As it turned out, it wasn't even a stranger who identified me but, of all people, my boy Zach's girlfriend, who had decided to cash in on the five-thousand-dollar reward and rat us out.

I was doomed.

Even without Robin's big mouth in the mix, it would have been just a matter of time before my boys and I were caught. After all, we had painted ourselves into a corner within the Houston metropolitan grid.

I was thrown into Harris County Jail with a bail of a hundred thousand dollars. I needed at least ten percent of that to get out. In other words, I was going nowhere and had no options.

Billie Jean visited me and acted like my counsel, giving me sisterly advice from her own brushes with the law. "I'm going to have my lawyer come and take care of you, Junior."

I listened to every word because, for some reason, she had been literally untouchable.

"Keep your head up, baby," she said before she left.

Even with Billie's encouragement, I felt like a lost child, especially while I was being interrogated. Just as you'd see on television, I sat at a small desk and the detectives did that good cop, bad cop thing. One acted like my friend, offering me creature comforts: "Do you want a smoke and some coffee?" The other made threats: "You're going to tell me what I need to know, or you're going away for a very long time."

I wasn't buying it. With a cold expression, I said, "I don't know what you're talking about. It wasn't me."

I almost got away with it. The consistency of my story and my refusal to cave made the prosecution's case a little more difficult to develop. Since I refused to take a plea, they had the burden of proof in the event of a trial.

While I feigned innocence, I bided my time in Harris County. To be honest, I didn't handle jail well at all. In fact, I had small anxiety attacks from the confinement.

I called Billie Jean, crying for her to get me out.

"Just calm down," she said. "The lawyer's working on things. Just make the best of your time."

As the weeks became months, I slowly but surely grew accustomed to jail and the daily routines of meals, recreation, showers—and obsessing over freedom. Every night in my bunk, I would fold my arms behind my head, stare at the gray concrete ceiling, and replay my arrest.

It was April 9, 1987, a fairly normal, sunny noontime in Houston. I went out with my girl, Red, a beautiful black-Asian sweetheart, for a romantic meal. After she and I parted ways, I met Zach at MacGregor Park. We spent the rest of the day doing our thing, selling and smoking weed. As the cool dusk settled in, I decided to head to my own place and crash for the night.

When I pulled up and parked at Willow Creek Apartments, something felt a little strange. Except for the wind rustling in the trees, the complex was eerily quiet. It looked deserted. As I walked toward my unit, it seemed as if a nuclear bomb siren had gone off hours before and I had missed it and been left alone to face the impact.

I knew it was time to calmly get into the apartment. A couple of regular-looking guys passed, but I didn't think much of it. As my little patio area came into view, I picked up the pace.

Something caught my attention. The giant maple tree that stood like a protective guard outside my front walk looked different in every way. I stopped and stared, and the sight chilled me.

From every imaginable angle, a swarm of cops materialized, looking like riot control for an unruly crowd of a hundred or more. The only things missing were helicopters buzzing overhead and SWAT team members rappelling down ropes. Every single cop was screaming. They engulfed me, pointing guns at my face, ready to blow my brains out.

When that million-mile-long arm of the law smashed me down to the ground, I knew this was it. I was taken straight to Harris County Jail for the beginning of a long and unforgettable journey.

I went through central booking, got my fingerprints taken, and stood for my mug shot. *It won't be long till this joke ends*, I thought as the camera snapped, capturing my ridiculous smile.

After the formalities, I was unceremoniously thrown into the general jail population. I shrugged it off. *Jail? How bad can it be?* I had always been able to adapt to my environment, and jail would be no exception.

The thirty-by-thirty-foot block had a television, small windows that let in very little sunlight, and several tables situated in the middle. My individual six-by-six-foot cell with its big iron door was one of about fifteen in the block. Everyone had a cell mate, or celly, and mine was a Spanish guy from Chicago named Peter, who was in for a murder beef. Peter was a cool cat, and we kicked it and got to know each other pretty well. We did a lot of push-ups together, which was inspiring to me because he was one big, muscular dude. I had a lot of respect for him.

Otherwise, there wasn't a whole lot to do but play chess, sit around and talk, or watch whatever was on the tube. For an hour a day, the guards let us outside on the hot, black-tarred roof, where we could play basketball. Since we didn't have the right shoes, we played in our bare feet, slipping and sliding, laughing hysterically.

Jail wasn't exactly the most traumatic place, but most of the time dragged. As a welcome break from the monotony, we would smoke joints when someone snuck weed in. Music was another escape. I hung out by our little radio box and became a bit of a musical connoisseur. Aside from R & B and classical stuff, country music of all things started appealing to me. Randy Travis in particular became one of my favorite artists.

Two of my partners in crime, Zach and Wendell, were also in Harris County. Locked up in there together, we had random chances to see each other during court appearances and such.

Those moments of seeing their familiar faces in such a strange place offered some comfort. In passing, we would nod at each other, make faces, and get in a few words.

Zach always tried to encourage me. "Man, fuck this shit, Book. We're gonna get you out of this, okay? You don't deserve to be in here. I got you, brother."

Zach was old school. He had gone through two prison bids and didn't want to see the system do to me what it had to him, breaking my life down, leaving me struggling to pick up the pieces over and over again. Zach was even willing to take the entire rap to help get me out, and that is something I will never forget. I mean, honestly, how many people would be willing to take on a possible extended sentence to help out a friend?

But as valiant as his efforts were, his testimony fell on deaf ears. Sure, the prosecutor's team listened to everything we all had to say, and they saw that my record had been clean, but they wanted all three of us to go down for this one.

After eight months, Harris County was wearing me down. I kept remembering my mother, who had passed when I was thirteen. Her lectures echoed in my head day and night: *Junior, you know right from wrong. There's no gray area in between. If you don't stop, you'll end up dead or in jail.* I came to accept that being locked up was my karma. I deserved it and could endure it free of resentment, and I wanted to do the right thing.

I began working with Gabe Niehaas, the attorney Billie had set me up with, to take a plea bargain. He was a tall, thin, white man with a chiseled face and a wealth of solid experience. I grew to respect and trust his counsel. He said I was making the best decision admitting guilt, and he informed me of one key factor: Judge Ted Poe.

Because I had been in Harris County long enough, I had seen many other guys' cases play out. The one thing they all feared was Judge Poe, who laid down the law on dudes just like me. His sentences were notoriously harsh. As much as I had prayed I would not get him, he was exactly the one I would be facing. Paranoia set in like quick-drying cement. I couldn't take any chances standing in front of that guy in a trial.

Gabe told me I had two choices. I could take a guilty plea for armed robbery and accept whatever sentence Poe felt was appropriate, or I could go to trial.

With all the evidence the prosecution had, including the eyewitness testimony and Robin's tip-off, a trial by jury would be suicide. Chances were I would be found guilty and face five to ninety-nine years. That meant I could be incarcerated for anywhere from ten to fifty years. I couldn't even fathom it.

Gabe worked with the prosecution and convinced them to allow me to plead guilty to two counts instead of all of them. In that case, I would be sentenced to five years for each, to run concurrently. It also meant if I was on good behavior, I could be out within eighteen to twenty-four months. It didn't take more than a minute for me to realize the plea bargain was the best offer that would come my way. I decided to take it.

The nine months I had now spent in Harris County counted as time served. I knew I would be looking at no more than another twelve to fourteen months in prison. I signed the necessary papers, admitting my guilt in black and white.

With all the worry about my fate now behind me, I could see my sentence as a chance to finally come to terms with my crime and concentrate on making a fresh start.

When the time came, I said my good-byes to all my homeboys and joined the chain gang of six or seven prisoners in shackles, handcuffs, and orange jumpsuits boarding the Texas Department of Criminal Justice bus.

Off we went to the unknown. I still had not been told which prison I would enter, and the road trip felt like a walk in the dark. My hands were sweaty, but I never let my nerves show. Inmates can smell fear and weakness a mile away, and I didn't want to open that Pandora's box. Before I knew it, we were pulling in to the Texas State Penitentiary at Huntsville, or Huntsville Unit, nicknamed The Wall because of the infamous old red brick walls erected in 1849.

Everyone going to prison in Texas went through The Wall for processing, or diagnostics, which is a basic set of checkups of blood, urine, dental work, and overall physical stature to evaluate each person's condition before he's sent to his final prison destination.

Although I would be at The Wall only one week, I quickly noted that jail and prison are very different things. When I first walked in, the meaning of it all overwhelmed me. There were four floors of cells, and an eerie feeling hung in the air. The Wall was and still is the most heavily used death row execution facility in the United States. I could almost taste the panic and death all around me. If ever a prison was haunted, The Wall is.

My cell was about eight-by-ten feet and contained a little steel toilet and a bunk bed. Crazy scribbles covered the wall, some dating back to the late seventies. I stared at those writings and got depressed. The gravity of how much of my life would be spent like this was indescribable.

I made sure to be pretty open around the other guys. I didn't want to come off as unfriendly or introverted, which could have landed me in trouble. You have to understand that in prison everyone is constantly sizing you up, determining how strong or weak your mentality is. It could mean the difference between being respected or preyed upon. It wasn't any different than the streets, which I knew plenty about. It's pretty simple, actually. If you handle yourself well, people will know not to get in your face.

It had never been hard for me to get along with everyone, no matter where I was. Besides, there wasn't much time to run into trouble with the other prisoners. We were on lockdown about twenty-two hours a day the week I was there.

For the most part, I had nothing to do other than get to know my celly. We had no outside or inside recreation, not even chess or dominoes. All we had was time. Time to eat, to shower, and to stare at the walls.

And stare and contemplate I did. I wondered where my

final prison stop would be. No one had told me anything. I was on a journey like Dorothy's in *The Wizard of Oz*, having been ripped away from the comforts of my home and sent on a trip among strange characters on a seemingly unending road. My road wasn't paved with yellow bricks but with gray concrete.

Finally my last day at The Wall came. At four in the morning, early enough to avoid the possibility of rousing other inmates and trouble, the guards escorted me and about twenty more prisoners through the dim halls. With one tiny bulb suspended a few dozen feet above us, I could see only the grim outline of each face.

I was relieved as we left behind the pungent air tinged by the regular use of the electric chair. As on my previous trip, I was shackled and led into an ominous old bus and cuffed to the seat. We pulled out of the confines of The Wall, leaving Huntsville permanently behind.

Since it was still dark, I couldn't see anything through the tinted and barred windows. It was still so early that I felt like a zombie in a foggy daze. My anxiety kicked in. Though no one said much, two of the guys were laughing, and I wondered, *How in the fuck can they be having a good time right now?* It must not have been their first ride to prison.

The trip in the blackness was a sixty-mile straight shot to Navasota, Texas. The bus made a turn onto Wallace Pack Road toward Pack 2, a work prison that held about fifteen hundred inmates serving for anything from arson to rape to armed robbery and murder. The day was breaking, and so was I.

Wide awake, I watched the intricate process as the bus entered the yard. The first razor wire gate opened, and we rode in and stopped while it shut behind us. A second gate released, and we pulled up to the main area. We were unlocked from our seats and led single file to the building. Armed guards were lined up as far as the eye could see on both sides.

Quickly I surveyed the surrounding outside areas, all woods void of leaves and life. It was January and cold even by Texas standards. The grounds were expansive and went a few hundred yards in each direction before hitting the tree line. Also visible on the outskirts of the property were a couple of rickety field houses where the guards must have lived.

Once inside I was unshackled, stripped, and given a cavity search. That was a real treat, let me tell you. Humiliating? Yes. Angering? Absolutely. Then I was taken to the laundry room and handed a blanket and my three sets of whites—my basic prison gear consisting of white shirts, pants, and sheets. I was responsible for keeping these cleaned and pressed at all times. Nothing was to be lost or stolen, or there would be penalties. As the guards rattled off the instructions, I tried to absorb the onslaught of information.

Once those procedures were taken care of, the rest of the new prisoners and I were led through a hall about half the length of a football field with the stalest of air like any old high school's. Bars separated us from the other inmates to the left and right.

All those dudes ran up to get a good look at us, talking smack and howling catcalls like, "Fresh meat!"

I kept real cool. These guys looked like any number of the people from the streets back home and didn't intimidate me in the slightest. In fact, a lot of them seemed desperate and down-trodden. However, some of the younger ones were obviously bitter and trying to hide behind false bravado. I didn't make eye contact with any of those dudes. I held my head high, where it was going to stay for the duration of my time at Pack 2.

I was led to my dormitory, which had a wide-open setup. Lined up in two neat rows were fifty racks, which are small beds with lockers at the end, just like in the military. Once I got to my rack, there weren't any formal introductions. The guard didn't have much to say other than, "This is prison. Mind your own business, and you'll be fine."

Thanks for the advice, I thought. *I already know that shit.*

Now it was just forty-nine strangers and me. The guys were hanging around their racks or milling about, talking and smoking cigarettes. Nobody bothered or paid any attention to me at all, which was fine. I wasn't paying any attention to them either. I stayed to myself. I was feeling defiant, but that was nothing new to me.

When I took a second to look around, I noticed the toilet right out in the open. When a guy had to do his business, he would do it in front of everybody, which was totally mortify-ing. You can imagine the sounds and smells. Sometimes people would crack jokes at some guy's expense while he sat on the bowl. Everyone would be dying laughing like a bunch of kids.

On the other end was a little area with a counter where dudes made coffee or "spreads." A spread was any variety of improvised snack made with items bought in the commissary or stolen from the kitchen. The guys would have canned goods like tuna or chicken, chili or stew, maybe packs of Ramen noodles, and then get creative making combinations. They might take the noodles, add some chicken and cheese, spice it up really well, and go to town. There were no limits to the variety guys came up with. Everyone considered himself to be a jailhouse chef with a definitive palate and an expert in the art of the spread. I would soon learn that those commissary items were worth their weight in gold. The prisoners regularly traded them for things like cigarettes, issues of *Playboy*, or joints.

My arrival was uneventful. It was a pretty quiet and calm unit, not to mention I was six foot two and two hundred pounds. All the other dudes could pretty much take one look and decide not to mess with me. I wasn't exactly a hard-ass or anything, but my expression was consistent and pretty serious. Had I been shifty, nervous, or afraid to look someone in the eye, he would have spotted it a mile away and tested me.

After taking all my gear to the rack, I tried to settle in. I made up the bed and put up a picture of Red. I had not seen her since my arrest in April, and now it was January. I lay there staring at the ceiling trying to wrap my mind around what had happened over the last nine months. This was the real deal. I was in prison. Real prison.

Thinking of Red and her excitement over my thug ways made me long for all those sleepless nights of smoking weed, counting drug money, and plotting the whole scheme that had landed me here. But I couldn't go back.

At around eleven that night the lights were shut off, but there was no way I was ready to go to sleep. With my rack sticking out between these concrete walls, I felt like I was lying in the middle of a hospital cafeteria. I was stuck with a herd of dudes snoring, whimpering, coughing, and sneezing—a symphony of annoyance in this room without a trace of light or hope.

Regret swirled in my head. *What the fuck did I get myself into?* At only twenty-two years old, I was a convicted felon feeling like I had just been erased from the world forever. I wanted to kick myself all over the place.

Even though the room was dark, I could see silhouettes of guys walking around doing their thing. Some sat in a small group passing a joint, quietly talking about getting back to the free world, while others made coffee and spreads. Just because it was lights-out didn't mean they had to sleep, so it was still business as usual for those who didn't want to lie quietly with their thoughts.

After I had stared at nothing and thought about everything for about an hour, my mind drifted back to my mother and those words that had haunted me since my first night in Harris

County Jail: *You'll end up dead or in jail.*

For the first time in years, I really missed her. I thought of the rest of my family too, my brothers and sisters. The story of our lives—together and divided, hellish at the time—played out in my mind as I nodded off to sleep.

BOOKER FROM THE BEGINNING

There were eight of us kids. In order from oldest to youngest, Mom had Danny James, Carolyn Jones, and Lula Gayle James, and then she had her five Huffmans—Billie Jean, Donald, Lash, Bonita, and me, Booker T, the mischief kid. I came into this world March 1, 1965, in Plain Dealing, Louisiana, born to Rosa and Booker T. Huffman. Yeah, I was Booker T. Huffman Jr. All my siblings called me Junior, but when my father suffered a stroke and died at the age of fifty-nine, I became the sole Booker T. Huffman. Still, out of habit and perhaps respect for our father, I would always be known to my immediate family as Junior.

Since I was only ten months old when Dad passed, I never had the chance to know him. The only thing I had of him was a photo showing a big, strong black man who looked like me. I used to focus on his frame and his face and wish I could be just like him.

Though I didn't know him for myself, everyone made it clear that he was a well-respected man. Fortunately, Carolyn, my oldest sister from one of Mom's earlier marriages, knew my dad for a few years before I was born and gave me insight into the man she called Mr. Booker.

"He was very quiet and rarely joked," she said. "But when he said something, you knew he meant it. We immediately did whatever he said. He was fairly tall, probably about six foot two, with a lean face, like yours. He always wore a khaki suit with a large-brimmed, beige hat made of felt. He looked like a hustler or a really slick man off the streets.

"One thing's for sure. Mr. Booker took care of our family. Mom stayed at home, and your father was a great provider, very responsible, a true man's man. We always had plenty of food and a nice place to live."

Once I asked Carolyn if she ever found out where Dad got his name, but she didn't know. That wasn't the only mystery. I didn't know what my middle initial stood for, if anything at all. I used to think it meant To-be-determined-at-a-later-time. No one could tell me. I do remember hating my name. Sometimes kids at school or around the neighborhood teased me, calling me Booger and things like that. For a while there I wanted to change it to something more typical, but as time went on I was proud to have something that set me apart and connected me to my father.

Carolyn's stories about him helped fill in so many blanks and were as therapeutic as they were entertaining. "I remember the first times your daddy came around when he started dating

Mama. He drove this big old green Oldsmobile that I used to call the Batmobile. Danny, Gayle, Don, and I loved to jump inside the Batmobile and horse around while Mr. Booker visited with Mom on the porch, just talking and laughing.

"He was such a pleasant man toward us kids and very generous. The local Dairy Queen sold a grape soda float called the purple cow. At least once a month, your father would load us all into the Batmobile and take us to get one. It was the thrill of the week! You never saw so much singing and dancing."

Soon my siblings would see a lot more of Mr. Booker. Carolyn told me, "One day he came over to Granddaddy Namon's house and asked him respectfully for Mom's hand in marriage. Of course Granddaddy said yes, and I'll tell you what, he and Mr. Booker were two peas in a pod from that day on. Mr. Booker gained a fine woman for a wife and a tremendous man for a best friend."

Carolyn's stories about my dad's job were fascinating too. "Mr. Booker used to work down at the local pool hall in Plain Dealing. It was a place where they served beer, played dominoes, and gambled some. That was your daddy's job six days a week from eight or nine in the morning until nine or ten at night. The only times he'd take off were Sundays to stay at home with Mama and us.

"On that seventh day, Sunday, he'd usually sit at the small kitchen table while Mama cooked one of her unbelievably delicious dinners. Mr. Booker would casually chat with her while counting his money for the week and then go sit out on the porch with Namon. The two of them had such a good time talking about life and the goings-on around town."

I loved hearing these stories. When I was old enough, Carolyn explained some funny details of my dad's seedier adventures. Apparently, another one of his Sunday activities was bootlegging with Granddaddy. It was illegal to sell liquor on Sundays, so he would buy a couple big bottles of whiskey, which they would sell little by little all day to make some pretty good side money. One time Dad got caught selling the whiskey to an undercover policeman, and they took him to jail.

When it was time for Dad to go to court, his defense attorney took one look at Granddaddy Namon and realized he could pull a switch. The crazy part was that even though the two of them dressed alike with the khaki suits and hats, Granddaddy was a light-skinned man and Dad was really dark. So to confuse things for the prosecutor, the lawyer had my granddaddy take the stand instead of my dad.

When the arresting officer came in to positively identify the man who had sold him the whiskey, the attorney pointed out Granddaddy. That policeman must have done a double take, and all of a sudden he wasn't so sure he had the right man. As a result, the judge had to throw the case out. The attorney had pulled the oldest trick in the book. Later at the house, Namon and my dad could be heard laughing into the wee hours of the morning about how they'd beaten the system.

In later years, Carolyn also went into detail about my dad's death. He was in great health, wasn't a drinking man, and never smoked, but on his way to work one day, he stopped off at one of those old icehouses to pick up a block for the pool hall. Suffering a stroke, he fell and died instantly in front of everyone.

It happened just shy of my first birthday in early 1966. There was no rhyme or reason to it. I guess it was just his time, as they say, but I sure wish it hadn't been.

Mom was beside herself with grief and concern for her family. Dad had been the breadwinner, and now she was left alone with a houseful of children to look after and feed. Almost immediately she looked for employment opportunities, and it wasn't long before she was hired as a medical assistant in town.

Although she worked long, hard hours, it wasn't enough. She needed a bigger, better opportunity. She called Carolyn, who had recently moved to Houston, to see how things were going out there.

"Great, Madea," Carolyn said, using our family's term of endearment for Mom. "There are so many jobs. You need to come and check it out for yourself. It could be a great move."

Though I don't remember anything about our town of Plain Dealing, I learned it offered nothing to us but dead-end jobs and racial tensions, even heavily segregated sections where black families had to live separately from whites. With such a bleak outlook, my mother was undoubtedly making a solid decision to move on.

After packing up a few things, she drove out to stay with

Carolyn while Granddaddy Namon and Gayle watched over the rest of us. Within a few weeks, Mom found a job as a nurse's assistant at the hospital as well as a house for rent in Sunnyside, a Houston suburb.

The next thing we knew, we were all crammed in her little red Plymouth and on our way to a new life.

Mom was a proud, hardworking woman. I had many wants, as most kids do, but because of her I didn't have any needs. We didn't have the sharpest car or the nicest house, but I had a coat on my back when it was cold, shoes on my feet, and hot meals on my plate even if it meant Mom had to take food stamps.

Mom worked from eleven at night till seven in the morning. She left when I was asleep, and she was home before I headed off to school. To my young mind, it seemed she had never left the house. I can't imagine how exhausted she must have been after a shift at the hospital to step into the kitchen to make us breakfast and pack our lunches. In the evenings, we would find her working hard in the kitchen again, smoking a Virginia Slims cigarette and maybe drinking a cold beer. None of us could wait to run in for dinner. Mom was an amazing cook. She had a big collection of recipes from former generations, and her mushroom chicken and candied yams were my favorite.

Raising eight children single-handedly must have taken its toll, but you would not have known it. Life at home with Mom was true peaches and cream. She cooked, cleaned, drove us wherever we needed to go, and expected nothing in return except that we would go to school and stay out of trouble.

From time to time, my sisters helped her out, but my brothers and I were lazy and never lifted a finger. All we wanted was to watch TV or bolt out the door and play.

By the time Danny, Carolyn, Gayle, and Billie Jean either had moved out or were running the streets, Mom was still taking care of Don, Lash, Bonita, and me. The four of us Huffman kids got along pretty well and didn't cause Mom too many headaches, but like any family we had our fights.

For some reason, I used to get into the most trouble, especially in school. I would have to guess that Dad's death translated into my acting out. Maybe seeing other kids with stable, two-parent homes triggered something deep inside. One thing was certain: Mom did not enjoy constantly being called down to the school to be lectured about her son's latest tirade.

One girl at school named Jackie had a crush on me. I never paid any attention, except to mess with her and call her names. One day, for whatever reason, I got the brilliant idea to bully Jackie for money.

"If you don't bring me five bucks tomorrow," I said, "I'll find you and make you sorry."

She was so shocked by my threats that she went home and stole the money from her mom's purse. She brought it the next day.

After school, I ran home chuckling over how easy my extortion plot had been. But then it dawned on me: I couldn't let Mom find out.

Nervously, I stashed the money outside. I had to come up with a story to explain the five dollars, or else I could never do anything with it. I thought up a plan and quickly set it in motion.

While I was playing with my little niece in the yard, I pulled out the cash. "Wow! Look what was just sitting here. I'm rich!"

I ran into the house and showed Mom my newfound wealth, and she bought my lie.

The next day I went to school thinking I had gotten away with the perfect crime.

My success was fleeting. As soon as I got to class, the teacher pulled me out and marched me to the principal's office. Jackie had reported my crime, and her mom had come all the way down to the school to complain. Everybody gave me the third degree, but that paled in comparison to what awaited me at home after they called my mother.

She whooped my ass. "Where'd you get such a crazy idea?" I really didn't know.

Then one day in third grade I lost my temper with the teacher and went crazy yelling, throwing books, and destroying anything in my way.

My mother came to meet me at the school. She put her hands on my shoulders and looked at me with her wide eyes. "Junior, why did you do this? What's the matter?"

I looked at her with a blank expression. I didn't have a reason to give. I really didn't know.

When I was still in grade school, we made a little move to

the west to an area called South Park, which would be my home for the next few years. I planted my roots and got used to the school and made some more friends.

Around this time, I started following my brother Lash when my friends weren't around to entertain me. Lash was six years older and much larger than me. In fact, he was one of the biggest kids around, and no one ever messed with him. He was also very protective of me. When we would walk in the neighborhood, his big palm would lightly clutch the back of my neck, while he guided me forward. It was his way of letting everyone know they would have to get through him to get to me.

I regarded Lash as a true role model and a hero I could always count on. There was nothing cooler than hanging out with him and his friends. Our age difference made us worlds apart in many ways, and I wanted to know more about his perspective of life. Lash was a giant of a teenager in a mysterious and private world of girls, fashion trends, and street knowledge. I went out of my way to sneak into Lash's business, but sometimes it was a bad idea.

Lash had a friend across the street named Clarence. We called him Brother, and he hung out with us most weekends. Some volatile fireworks were usually going off at his house. His dad was a hardworking man, and when Friday afternoon arrived, he drank as hard as they came. Every so often when we were at his house, we would notice Clarence's mom had a black eye or a swollen cheek. It was no surprise Brother sought escape from all that by spending time with Lash and me.

As good of a friend as Brother was to me, Lash was closer to his age and had the much stronger tie. Those two did everything together, and I always tagged along, even when they didn't want me to. Of course, I did everything possible to secretly follow.

One afternoon, when I had walked behind them all the way down the street, my brother turned around and noticed me. "You ain't coming," he yelled, and they took off running as fast as they could to ditch me.

"Yes, I am," I hollered and gave chase. But I just couldn't keep up. I ran so hard I fell in the street. I cried like a baby, part of me hoping Lash would see me and come back. When he didn't, I finally stood up and ran to find them. Lash saw me and threw his hands up. He let me stay, but I soon wished he hadn't.

Walking aimlessly, we eventually found a stray cat. Lash and Brother decided to catch him. I can't remember if the cat was overly friendly or if they had some food or something to lure him, but they wound up bagging the little guy.

Cat in tow, we started walking again. From my place behind the older boys, I couldn't really hear what they were talking about, but that poor cat was crying and I could see him struggling to get out. We got to the end of our street, then crossed a few more blocks until we were near Interstate 610. Beneath the freeway was an underpass where we always hung out when we didn't have anything better to do.

While I wondered where we were going or why we still had the cat, Lash and Brother climbed the embankment near the freeway. As cars whizzed by, the boys laughed and the cat battled. Then in a sudden thrust, my brother flung the bag as high as he could into the oncoming traffic.

Miraculously, instead of being hit by any of the speeding cars, the cat landed on the double yellow lines of the freeway, managed to crawl out of the bag, and sat there paralyzed with fear. When he suddenly made a break for it, an eighteen-wheeler hit him, crushing his tiny skull. His mouth was twisted and warped beyond recognition.

"Whopped Mouth," my brother said in his heavy Texas drawl. Warped Mouth. I'm sad to say I knew exactly what he meant.

We used to race slot cars at a shop in Pasadena that had this huge track. Kids from all over came for tournaments. Lash was especially obsessed with that place and was there front and center every weekend.

What I remember most about the shop isn't the racing at all. It's an old worker. My brother had it in for this guy. Probably in his late sixties, the man had a hideously contorted face. His visage definitely wasn't the most pleasant thing to look at, especially his mouth. He didn't seem to have a trace of a jaw on the left side.

I tried not to pay any attention to this man, but Lash was obsessed with making fun of him. From the moment we headed out our door until we walked inside the hobby shop, during the slot car races, and all the way back home, Lash laughed about this guy and called him all kinds of names: The Elephant Man,

Droopy, and his favorite—Whopped Mouth.

"Whopped Mouth," he yelled. "That guy's got a fuckin' whopped mouth."

And there it was. As hard as I tried to forget that cat, Lash sure would not let me. After that day at the freeway, every time we went to race slot cars and Lash started up the jokes, that cat would come to mind. Even if my brother didn't say anything but I saw that guy at the shop, that poor cat was at the forefront of my thoughts. It was a terrible association, but once it was there, it was permanent.

That whole situation changed my perspective of Lash, but I forgave him and let it go. He was still my big brother and hero.

Lash and I always played together, using our imaginations to transform even rainstorms into opportunities for fun. We ran to the street where the rainwater flowed like a river down the curb to the drain about fifty yards away. We loved to race matchsticks. Lash gave me a burnt match, and I was the mysterious Racer X from the *Speed Racer* cartoon. With his clean match, he was Richard Petty, number forty-three, the NASCAR champ.

"Ready, set, go!" We put the matches in the water, and our race began. The only real rule was that if your match got stuck on the way, you could tap it with your finger to get it going into the current again.

To me it was just a fun game, and I don't remember winning a single one of those races. But to Lash, everything was a serious competition. That was one big difference between us.

When he raced slot cars at the shop, Lash was a young man possessed. It was all so exciting to him, and it was impossible to get his attention when he was preparing his car for action. It was pretty cool to see these little plastic cars doing forty-five to fifty miles per hour on those big guided tracks filling up the room. All along the edges kids and grown men alike hollered while their cars were in hot pursuit.

Lash raced in tournaments for hours on the weekends, always imagining himself to be Richard Petty. I wondered why he didn't go for Willy T. Ribbs, the black NASCAR driver, but the answer was pretty simple: Petty always won.

Being there made me happy, but I didn't take that scene as seriously as my brother did. It was enough for me to race my little car on the smaller, less competitive tracks, avoiding Whopped Mouth at all costs.

When we weren't at the race track or getting into trouble, we were with the family. At Thanksgiving, Don, Lash, Bonita, and I crammed into the Chevy Malibu for the long haul to Louisiana to see my grandparents. Our holidays together were boisterous. The real show came Christmas Day, when our older siblings, Danny, Carolyn, Gayle, and Billie Jean arrived bearing gifts and showing off their sense of seventies high fashion.

Gayle pulled up in her Cadillac Eldorado, stepped out like a movie star, and strolled to the front door as if she were on the red carpet for a Hollywood premiere. We oohed and ahhed over her grand entrance.

Billie Jean could be heard coming a mile away. When I heard her stereo blaring, I ran to the window and watched her slink out of the driver's seat with a red dress so tight it looked painted on.

Carolyn, on the other hand, was way more casual with her clothing. She nonchalantly walked in with a green skirt and a nice button-down shirt. She was not fooling anyone, though. A fire burned behind those dark brown eyes.

Little did I realize how much my siblings' lifestyles would influence me.

STREET EDUCATION

As I got older, I realized some of my siblings were true rogues of society. By observing them, I made fascinating discoveries about the world around me. One revelation came a month and a half after I turned eleven. I guess Mom saw me, her baby boy, growing into a little man and decided I should get my very first suit in time for Easter Sunday. Since Carolyn was around that weekend, Mom asked her to take me shopping while she prepared for everyone's arrival.

Carolyn drove us to the department store. As soon as we got there, I made a beeline to the children's section. I found my new outfit right away: a brown suit with pinstripes. Man, that getup reminded me of gangster movies. I went to a mirror and held it up, imagining how cool it would look on me.

"Did you find what you were looking for? Come on." She looked at the ceiling and all around before grabbing my hand. "Let's go try it on."

I went into one of the stalls, took off all my clothes, and put on the suit. Perfect fit. I stepped out to show Carolyn.

She smiled. "Okay, Junior, now put your clothes on over the suit."

What? I didn't get it, but within seconds we were both tugging on my jeans, shirt, and jacket until the suit was totally concealed. My clothes puffed out so much I looked like a World War II–era deep-sea diver. On top of that, I was itching like crazy.

All I could think was, *Whoa, my sister's a booster.* Even though I was a little nervous, the idea of stealing the suit was somewhat exhilarating. Being so haphazardly thrown into Carolyn's world made me feel grown-up and cool. Sure, it was wrong. Sure, my mother would have slapped me upside the head if she was there, but that was exactly what made it so great.

"Just keep cool and don't act like anything's wrong," Carolyn said. "The last thing we want is to look suspicious and give ourselves away. Follow me to the front doors and walk straight to the car."

Scared out of my mind, I made the long trek from the dressing area to the exit, my eyes glued to Carolyn's back. I completely expected a security guard to grab my shoulder, and my heart practically pounded out of my chest. When we hit the doors and my feet touched the asphalt, I let out a sigh.

Carolyn didn't say a word. During the ride home, though, as I slunk out of my street clothes to reveal my free suit, I saw a little smirk on her face.

Back at the house, Mom fawned over her little man and posed me for a picture.

BOOKER T. HUFFMAN

I looked in the mirror and marveled. *Not bad. Booker T. Huffman, eleven-year-old master criminal.*

Carolyn stood there grinning, and I could barely keep from bursting out laughing. My career had only begun.

After our little heist, apparently Carolyn knew I was cool and could keep a secret, so she let her guard down around me. Sometimes she helped Mom by taking my sister Bonita and me to her house. Anything could happen at her place anytime—and it usually did.

There was no denying the strength of Carolyn's influence on me. The idea of taking what I wanted when I wanted it really appealed to me. It wasn't long before I struck again, solo this time—or at least I tried to.

One weekend when Bonita and I visited her house, Carolyn needed to run some errands. She took us to the Laundromat and loaded the machine. After clinking in a couple of quarters, she suggested we go out for a bit. "My friend lives right across the street. You'll have fun playing over there."

Bonita and I just shrugged and followed, as always.

Almost immediately after we stepped into her friend's house, Carolyn disappeared into some other room. Bonita and I ran around and made the best of things, like all kids do, losing track of time and having not a care in the world.

Eventually Carolyn came out with a strange expression and bloodshot eyes. She seemed a little disoriented.

I guess she's just tired, I thought.

"Let's get our clothes and get back home," she said, leading us out the front door and across the street.

Bonita and I played while Carolyn finished her load. It was getting dark out when she emerged with her basket of clothes. As we followed her to the car, she stumbled and spoke gibberish. I dismissed it and jumped into the backseat.

None of us wore seat belts as we cruised through the neighborhood. Lost in thought, I stared at the passing houses.

Out of nowhere I heard a crunch and nose-dived into the back of the passenger seat. I didn't know what had happened, but my instincts kicked into overdrive.

Bonita was wedged like a doorstop into the space between the two front seats. I grabbed her and got her out. She was crying and nearly hyperventilating but was otherwise okay.

I ran to the driver's side. Carolyn had smashed her head into the steering wheel and was moaning. She pulled me in close. "Here, take this and put it away somewhere for me." She placed a .38-caliber revolver in my hand.

Without even thinking about it, I slid the gun into one of my cowboy boots, which I always wore back then, and stayed by Carolyn's side.

As a result of the huge commotion, all the locals started pouring out of their houses to see what was going on. It turned out Carolyn had hit a car parked at the curb.

Soon the cops came speeding in, lights on and sirens blaring. I was scared my sister would get in big trouble and have to go to jail or something, but things back then were so much different. *Really different.*

Carolyn explained that she had looked away from the road for a split second and hadn't seen the other car.

And you know what? The cops did not suspect her of being intoxicated. They must have thought she was simply disoriented from the crash. They never searched her and didn't even give her a ticket.

By then, Carolyn's friend from down the street had arrived and offered to drive us back to South Park.

When I slipped my sister her .38, she smiled and winked.

Just as we had with our little heist, we kept the whole thing secret and acted is if it had never happened.

Secrecy began to saturate my way of thinking. It became a code to live by. Although I didn't realize it at the time, the behavioral patterns of my siblings were taking hold and starting to weather and mature me. My paramount ideals were to never get caught for any kind of scheme and, if I did, to keep my mouth shut and deny everything.

As my education continued to develop, I tested myself. I thought the more I risked, the greater the reward would prove to be. There was no guarantee things would work out. All I had was the blind faith that I would emerge on the other side still shining and maybe carrying a few extra bucks in my pocket.

I soon had my first real opportunity to put my newfound philosophies into practice. Every other month, this white man came through my South Park neighborhood to peddle his own scheme. One afternoon he told me the deal. He employed young kids to sell flowers on the street corners in exchange for a tiny percentage of the profits. The arrangement was a five-dollar take for every fifty dollars sold.

Man, a kid with five bucks was rich! I figured, *Why not?* Of course, this would have to be a secret Booker T adventure. I quickly meditated on my new mantra: *Say nothing to anyone; deny everything if caught.* Then I was on my way.

The guy drove me about half an hour away. I was pretty damn scared. Sure, I tried to be mature and fearless, but under the facade I was still just a kid.

Finally, the man dropped me off on a busy street corner in this all-white area called Bellaire and handed me a huge bundle of flowers. "I'll be back in an hour or two to check on you, okay?"

I nodded, and he sped off.

With a stomach full of butterflies, I stood there questioning what in the world I was doing.

The guy knew what he was talking about, though. Before long, I had sold all my stock. I guess the little downtrodden black boy and his bouquets of flowers pulled the heartstrings of all those upper-crust white folks driving by. Maybe they thought it was their good deed of charity for the year. Those suckers. It was the perfect ploy.

True to his word, the salesman returned. "Holy shit, kid, you did great." He speedily unloaded another pile of flowers on me and said he'd be back.

I felt great. I was making my own way in a daring situation. I'd land in a boiling pot of trouble if my mother only knew. This held the excitement and danger of the adventures of boosting the suit and holding Carolyn's .38 rolled into one.

Eventually I ran out of flowers again, but this time the dude did not return as scheduled. As evening fell, panic set in. I knew my mother was probably wondering where I was, and I just wanted to get home as soon as possible. I waited and hoped the salesman would show up and drive me home to South Park. Surely he would make good, especially since I had all his money.

Finally I started thinking of how to help myself instead of waiting around. Maybe a stranger would be willing to help. I ran to the gas station across the street to see if someone would give me a ride or let me use the phone. Even though I had a pocketful of about eighty dollars from the flower sales, I was too scared to use it. What if the guy came back and got mad?

The whole thing was really wearing me down, and I knew my bluff had been called. I was not a seasoned hustler. I was just a rattled little kid lost in a strange place.

I approached the gas station at the far corner. This guy casually rode up on a bike and parked it against the side of the store. Fairly nondescript, wearing a black hooded sweatshirt and jeans, he strolled inside. He was probably buying a pack of cigarettes or a Hostess Honey Bun for all I knew or cared. While I was still standing there confused about my predicament, the dude came walking out, got on his bicycle, and pedaled into the distance.

Within minutes, cops stormed in from all directions with the lights going, sirens blaring—the works. The gas station had been robbed right in front of me. The place turned into a mob scene of commotion, law enforcement, and a frightened little Booker T.

As far as robberies go, this was not at all what I had expected. There had been nothing physical, no shouting. The clerk had not even chased the guy to get a good look at him.

I, on the other hand, was totally overwhelmed and made a scene of my own. I broke down right then and there. This little big man had been reduced to a baby in less than thirty seconds flat. Some of the officers noticed and began questioning me. After I told them the little I had seen, which didn't help at all, they left me alone with my tears and panic.

Fortunately, a nice old white lady was pumping gas and took pity on me. She called my mother on the pay phone and waited with me until Mom pulled up.

Although I was relieved to see Mom, when I noticed the look of death on her face, it dawned on me how much trouble I was in. When we got home, I told her everything that had happened, shattering my unbreakable street code. I hoped the truth would make things easier on me.

Soon after I told her the story, the phone rang. It was the salesman. He wanted to stop by to pick up his money for the flowers. My mother told him to come on by, but her voice sent a message: *I dare you to show up at my house.*

The dude opted to never show up at all, and Mom simply kept the entire eighty bucks.

We never spoke of my brief sales career again. Some businessman I was! I hadn't even gotten my commission. Though it was an expensive punishment, I was just thankful I hadn't gotten a whooping.

About that time, my mother started dating a man named Robert Hill, a self-employed carpenter and fisherman. Every so often, he'd take me to the beach to be his assistant. He let me do a little fishing of my own, which was a welcome escape for a city kid like me. Times with Robert were pretty cool, and I slowly started to see him as a father figure, especially when he and Mom got married. Then suddenly, for reasons I was too young to understand, they were divorced and he was gone, leaving Mom on her own again to take care of us kids.

On March 1, 1978, I turned thirteen. What could have been a symbolic entrance into manhood turned into a nightmare. As I mentioned, my mom worked nights, then sent us off to school with breakfast in our bellies and lunches in our backpacks. The rest of her late mornings and early afternoons were probably her only time to unwind and grab a little sleep while the house was quiet. Once we crashed through the door all hyped up from a day of school, she was on her feet and busy again. While we turned on the television, made snacks, and ran around tormenting each other, she vacuumed, picked up after us, and made dinner. It was great having Mom there to take care of things. It seemed like it would last forever, but it didn't.

Nothing special was going on in our house this particular afternoon. We all did our thing, decompressing while waiting to eat. Mom cleaned up and did the laundry. While all of us pretty much just lay in her way, Mom went to the hall to turn the attic fan on.

Most houses in South Park had attic fans. We weren't fortunate enough to have true air-conditioning. The big blades in the middle of the attic wall resembled an airplane propeller. When turned on, they sucked up all the stale air through the vents and propelled it outside. Unfortunately, even with the windows open, the circulation delivered a brick wall of hot, dry air. But sometimes if there was a nice breeze through the windows, we gained a steady cross flow that cleared out the dusty Texas air.

When Mom noticed the fan wasn't working that afternoon, she asked if anyone would go check it out. The thing about checking the fan was that you actually had to go up to the attic, which was ridiculously dark and dangerous. The key to a safe visit was to concentrate while carefully walking along the top edges of the wooden crossbeams, which were horizontal drywall supports on the other side of the living room ceiling. A dozen rows of beams, separated by two-foot gaps, went from one end of the house to the other. The only flooring in between was fiberglass insulation and a thin layer of Sheetrock.

I always found going up there to be a scary proposition and

avoided it at all costs. A chore of that caliber was almost always met with a look of *Who, me?* from anyone within Mom's line of sight, and this time was no exception. Mom shook her head, pulled the drop ladder down, and slowly disappeared into the attic.

Without any warning but a quick, shrill scream, Mom crashed through the ceiling.

In shock, I watched her fall about ten feet straight down onto her neck and back.

No one knew what to do except panic.

Though Mom had seriously injured her back, she didn't let the pain show. I guess she felt it was important to maintain her composure for our sake. When Bonita started crying a little bit, Mom said calmly, "Don't worry. I'll be okay."

Haunting words if ever there were any.

One of my brothers ran to the phone to dial 911. When the ambulance arrived, we all jumped in by her side for the trip to the hospital. Because of my mother's reassurances, it still did not seem all too scary. When we got to the hospital, Mom was rushed away, and we were left to wait.

Although still shaken up, I was restless while I sat and stared at the wall. After hundreds of slow-crawling minutes, all our siblings arrived and we gathered to discuss what had happened.

When the doctor finally came out, the older members of the family spoke with him off to the side.

Billie Jean approached Bonita and me and told us Mom was stable, whatever that meant, and would be okay. She had some kind of damage to her back and would need surgery. "Routine procedure," she said. "They just need to go in and remove some of the fluid that came out of her slipped discs."

Again I was left in the dark.

Mom's operation was an apparent success. While she recovered, we visited her all the time. She smiled and gave out kisses and asked us to catch her up on the goings-on in our lives and at the house. I told her everything was fine and that Don and Lash kept an eye on Bonita and me and that Carolyn and Billie Jean regularly checked in as well.

All in all, life seemed pretty normal. We got used to Mom being laid up in the hospital, thinking all along she would be home any day. Finally, after waiting and wondering for what felt like an eternity, we saw Mom walk right through our front door.

As would be expected, she moved a little slower, but there she was. That very first night she picked up right where she had left off, cooking one of her amazing dinners. It was almost as if nothing had changed when we sat down to the table to eat her famous mushroom chicken.

After a few months of normalcy, however, things got complicated. My mother experienced numbness in her legs, and during her recommended therapy it became clear something was not right. My sisters said they had a bad feeling about where all this might be headed.

I chose to ignore them. *Madea will be all right*, I thought. *She's got to be.*

Mom finally went back to the doctor to explain what she was feeling. After a battery of tests, she learned that the remaining fluid in her spine was compressing against a nerve, causing slight paralysis in her legs and feet. She needed one more corrective procedure to remove fluid and relieve the pressure. Then all would be well.

Mom was not thrilled at all about going under the knife again but reluctantly agreed, hoping for a normal life. On the day of her surgery, we all came to the hospital to show our support. We gathered around the bed to wish her luck, and I gave her a big kiss and a hug.

Before the nurses came, Mom repeated her soothing assurance. "Don't worry, Junior. I'll be okay."

As far as I was concerned, my mother's word was gospel. If Mom said she would be okay, I had to believe it.

About an hour later, most of us kids were outside playing football to pass the time. Billie Jean came frantically running out the hospital doors. When she finally got close and flagged us down, she struggled to speak. "There was a problem with Madea's surgery. The doctor said they had an unexpected complication, and she stopped breathing. Now she's in a coma and on life support."

A chill ran up my arms and down my spine.

When I finally saw my mother, she simply appeared to be sleeping. Aside from having her eyes closed and being hooked up to a breathing machine, she still looked the same. Maybe if she'd had some sort of obvious external injury, it would have immediately registered with me. As far as I knew, Mom would wake up in a couple of days.

She never did.

The days passed and Mom showed no signs of improvement whatsoever. She had zero brain activity and was kept alive with an oxygen ventilator and a nutrition tube.

A few weeks later, my brothers and sisters gathered to talk about what to do. Because Mom had never designated power of attorney to anyone and did not have a living will, the family would have to determine how to handle the situation and all of Mom's affairs.

Although I did not want to hear it, they decided the only choice remaining was to remove Mom from life support. We were told we would have to go to court to gain permission, which did not sit well with any of my older siblings because the process would cost a lot of money and time. They were not interested in any of that and could not have afforded it.

When it came down to it, we made the group decision to pull the plug ourselves.

With silence hanging heavily in the air, we slowly filed into her room. None of us knew what to do or say. It felt like time stopped altogether.

I stared around the room, looking to my siblings for comfort. All I found was confusion. The truth is that each of us was just as lost as the other. There was no way to escape the crushing pain. We were forced to face it as a group and then deal with it individually over time.

Just as Danny and Gayle approached the tubes and wires, the doctor walked in and decided to do it himself. We all took one last look at our beautiful, forty-nine-year-old mom, held her hand, and told the doctor we were ready.

As he went to work removing the mask and unplugging the equipment, the room filled with loud beeps and warnings.

Panic flashed through me. Horrified, I looked at everyone else, wishing the chaos would stop. I felt like I was paralyzed and slowly drowning as, with each second, my mom faded further away.

The beeping fell flat, and the heart rate monitor traced a glowing straight line. Rosa Huffman, my beautiful mother and only dependable guide, was gone. I had no idea how I would cope without her.

ON MY OWN

My mom's passing struck an instant division in the family and inside me. Everyone ran around wondering what to do in the void our mother had left behind, and no one had any concrete ideas. I was only thirteen years old, but my carefree, protected life was over.

I grieved for my mother tremendously, but at first her death did not affect me as deeply as you would expect for someone so young. Unprepared to grasp what had happened in that room, I was resentful. When it came to confronting my feelings, I just didn't.

We made all the necessary arrangements through Carolyn's boyfriend, Luther Johnson, a respectable businessman who had the means. Luther owned a funeral parlor and took care of everything, leaving one less worry for us during such a difficult time.

It was not until the actual funeral that everything really hit me. I was not prepared to see my mother in a casket. In my lifetime, I had seen only one person at rest—my grandmother Ms. Odie James—and I was too young to feel the impact.

However, when Bonita and I saw Mom's body, her expressionless face, and her closed eyes, we were both so upset we had to look away immediately, tears streaming uncontrollably down our cheeks.

Various members of our extended family and some of my mother's friends filed in and out, paying their last respects and offering condolences.

We got into our cars, formed a short motorcade, and followed the hearse to the cemetery in Plain Dealing, where a minister read some prayers. As two caretakers began to lower Mom's coffin into the plot beside the graves of other deceased family members, I walked to the edge and looked down. I tossed in a handful of dirt and said a final good-bye.

My life would never be the same.

While I fought grief, my family fought each other. In fact, the whole time Mom had been in the coma, my siblings had been constantly doing one of two things: consoling each other or arguing about what to do with Bonita and me. The rest of them were old enough to take care of themselves. I had never even thought about living anywhere but home. What kid does? You wake up, go to school, and go home. Now, in the midst of trying to cope with such a great loss, this worry hit me like a sledgehammer.

Aunt T., Mom's sister who was her spitting image, made it known that she really wanted to take on Bonita and me. Well, I guess this possessive thing came over my sisters because they did not like that idea at all. They went back and forth arguing, making it clear to Aunt T. that we were not going with her anywhere. My sisters' stance was that Aunt T.'s taking custody and moving Bonita and me across the state would tear the family apart. Carolyn and Billie Jean stepped up and said they would look after us, insisting it was the only way to ensure our lives would go on as they had before.

I had a sinking feeling. What would become of Bonita and me? The two of us felt like rag dolls in a game of tug-of-war, pulled apart at the seams. Danny and Gayle were gone without much of a trace, and slowly but surely everyone else bailed too. Though Carolyn and Billie Jean had told Aunt T. they would look after us, Bonita and I wound up going back to our house in South Park.

For a while, my nineteen-year-old brother Lash and twenty-five-year-old brother Don were still there.

Don came and went from the house, working odd jobs and not paying attention to Bonita or me, let alone lifting a finger to help out. Maybe he only stayed to avoid paying rent somewhere else. In some ways, I think he had never really adjusted to Texas life after moving from Louisiana. Having no true ties in Houston, Don probably struggled to put the pieces of his uprooted life back together. Ultimately, Don picked up and moved on, leaving us behind.

Lash never said anything about his feelings, but the deterioration of everything around us wreaked havoc on him too. There was no feeling of the family or security everyone had promised.

Bonita and I tried to live as we had before, waking every

weekday morning, going to school, and coming home to play or watch television. When we got hungry, though, there was never any dinner and we had to scrape and salvage any canned and dry food left in the kitchen. Dry cornflakes and cans of cold beans now replaced Mom's delicious cooking. Once in a while, Carolyn or Billie would bring a few things to eat or some fast food, but then they were gone for days in a row.

I truly believe Billie had it in her heart to be a motherly figure. As much as she may have imagined herself to be the one who would step up and champion our cause, she just was not capable. She was not ready to slow down and play house.

Things felt really bleak, and I was becoming more depressed and withdrawn. Our life slowly ran down into a sad state. It never seemed to dawn on anyone that the bills weren't getting paid. Utilities were shut off one by one, starting with the electricity. Our once-thriving home was now just an empty, dark house with no soul.

One day I came home from school and noticed Lash's things were gone. His car, his clothes, and even his toothbrush were nowhere to be found.

A night passed, then another, and still there was no sign of my brother. Finally I found out that Lash had decided to lead an entirely new life that didn't include Bonita or me. He was literally down the street from our house, living with a buddy of his.

I was disappointed to be in the midst of a systematic family desertion. It was not difficult to understand why Lash had disappeared, but I was upset he had not reached out to us, invited us to dinner, or acknowledged us around town and school.

Occasionally I took the initiative to visit him at his friend's house, which made the whole thing even stranger. Although his friend's family was really nice, they didn't ask about Bonita's and my home life or lack thereof. On one or two occasions, they invited us in when we stopped by to see Lash, but that was the extent of things. I never felt more alone than when I left their house, knowing Lash was inside, apparently trying to forget all about his previous life.

I couldn't understand why we were alone in a cold, unforgiving house. Things went from bad to worse to hell and beyond. It got to the point that almost every day brought a new obstacle for us to find some way over, under, or around. Without electricity, we depended on candlelight during those cruel nights. Sometimes we would even pray for a full moon to illuminate the darkness.

It was as if we were wishing on a fallen star. In the end, it was our hope that had fallen. We never knew what to expect. One day we would wake up and discover there was no running water. The next we would come home and find the gas had been shut off. Our yard was overgrown. The municipality did not pick up our trash even when we did set it out, so garbage was everywhere. The house was becoming extra creepy with its pungent odor, like some stranger's shack we had been thrown into after being kidnapped. It was disgusting and terrifying.

I wanted my mom. Our brothers and sisters had sworn to

take us in and give us love, protection, and guidance, but they'd failed us. It was all I could do not to sit and cry with Bonita, looking at the spot in the ceiling where our mother had crashed through. I daydreamed about setting the house on fire and running away with Bonita, but we had no place to go. We were stuck.

Some cloudy days had a little silver lining. A guy next door who knew what was happening would use a little street ingenuity to turn our utilities back on, but it was always temporary. The phone and electric companies caught wind of it and shut off their services, but we still appreciated this man's kind attempt.

Other than that, while all the neighbors in our area knew about the trouble Bonita and I were facing, no one came around to check in on us. It was disheartening. In the movies or on television, I had seen the family with a mother who passed away and left behind an emotionally crippled and helpless widower with his confused children. Then there would be a knock at the door, and in would walk the neighbors with pots and pans of food to help in their time of need. That sure wasn't the scenario in South Park in 1979.

Left to manage on our own, Bonita and I ate whatever we could find. By now we had no trash bags, so the garbage-ridden house became infested with roaches and pests. Rats crawled at our feet. Still no one showed their faces at our door, and I thought maybe we'd just die there unnoticed.

Day after day, night after night, the two of us fended for ourselves. Now that we were relying on only each other, we effectively forged into one person with two sets of eyes keeping watch. At night, we hid in bed in the shadows, frightened out of our minds at the prospect of someone with insidious intent lurking around the corner. Even though we had nothing worth taking, anyone could have easily broken in. To us, every little sound was a thief, a kidnapper, or a murderer.

We certainly did not go completely without violation in our home. One night, Billie Jean swung by to see how we were. She casually looked around, not seeming too concerned with the dilapidated conditions until she noticed one thing.

"Where's the television set?" she yelled. "Bonita, Junior, where the hell is the TV set?"

I was startled. I honestly had not noticed it was gone. After all, the electricity had been out for months. Now that Billie brought it up, we quickly realized we had been ripped off. Years before, the television had been a gift from Billie and one of her sugar daddies. He was a great guy who owned a car dealership and lived to please my sister. In all reality, he was just a married sucker Billie was using, like all the other men she had wrapped around her finger.

One day my sister had influenced him to buy my mother a forty-inch television complete with a remote control. We were blown away when he wheeled it in and it glowed for the first time. It would replace our small black-and-white set with its twisted wire-hanger bunny ears and pliers attached to the knobs for changing channels. This new TV was the most valuable possession in our house. Billie was so proud of herself for giving Mom and us something nice to enjoy.

Now Billie stood in our dim living room screaming. "It was Robert Hill!" She looked around frantically. "I'm going out. You two stay put."

Robert Hill? Up until then, the only thoughts I'd had of my former stepfather were of our good times fishing. Now he'd been tiptoeing around, stealing from us and his deceased ex-wife? The whole thing was disgusting to imagine.

He was in trouble now. The last thing you wanted to do was cross Billie. She was hotheaded and tough as nails, and she always carried her pride and joy, the Dirty Harry Callahan–style .44 Magnum, in her purse.

I later learned she put the word out on the street and did some investigating. When she found out Robert Hill had in fact broken in and stolen the set, she wasted no time tracking him down and confronting him with her .44.

"You motherfucker, you broke into my house and stole the TV I gave Madea? You better run!"

As he tried to flee in his car, she blasted a few shots right through his windshield.

Miraculously, he ducked and swerved out of the way, literally dodging bullets that would have blown his conniving head clean off.

In true Billie style, although the cops came and grabbed her, she ended up with only an assault charge. She was in a holding tank overnight, but nothing could stick to that girl. She casually strolled out of there the next morning, knowing Robert Hill would never, ever come around and mess with the Huffmans again.

Back at the house, life was getting more insane. Things were heating up Texas summer style, and we were completely out of water. Bonita and I thought about it a while and made a plan. We looked around the house and gathered fifteen water bottles to fill at the local gas station.

But there was an issue. The gas station was only a quarter of a mile down the road, but we had too many bottles to carry. *We're fucked*, I thought. Or were we?

Over the last year or so, our family had come and gone and left us behind, taking everything in the house with them as they went. Interestingly, though, one item remained: my mom's old Chevy Malibu. I guess my siblings thought it was junk, but I didn't. I saw it as the last real piece of my mother still standing and ready to help us on our way.

The Malibu had definitely seen better days. Even though it ran, it could not go in reverse. That little detail did not make a bit of difference to me. Bonita and I ran out and loaded the backseat with the bottles, and I cranked up the engine, which backfired so loudly people must have thought there was a shooting. Down the street we went on a wing and a prayer.

The whole way there, I kept thinking, *What am I doing? I'm not old enough to drive, and here I am risking life and limb for the both of us—just to get water!*

That rickety old car made good to the station, though, and we bailed out and commenced filling our containers. I felt totally demoralized and wondered what people thought of these two kids jumping out of a car and filling up one bottle after another. In the end, what they might have thought didn't matter. The important thing was that we now had something to drink and wash ourselves with.

When we had filled every container, we were ready to go. Since the car couldn't go in reverse, I asked Bonita to get in and steer while I pushed the car backward. She maneuvered a K-turn. Then, out of breath, I jumped in and started it up. We blasted off with that backfire and puttered all the way back to our lifeless hovel.

We made it home unscathed with our cache of gas station tap water. You would've thought we'd just scored a full-scale dinner with trimmings and all the soda we could drink.

Even with a success like that to keep us going, our hope faded again. Something had to give. So many mortgage bills had gone unanswered, and the bank had sent dozens of foreclosure and eviction warnings. Finally, after seeing all this, Carolyn stepped in and brought us to her place until she could decide with the family what to do with us.

It was at this point that I realized just how serious everything was. For the first time in my young life, depression started to settle in. I was spinning with confusion. Bonita stayed fairly calm and collected, though like me she probably wanted to break down.

I thought about how my sisters had battled with Aunt T. over our custody, claiming they wanted to keep the family together. If the past year had been any indication of what they meant by keeping us together, I would have rather run away and hopped on a train car or something. At least the hobos probably would have shared their rotten, oily sardines with me.

When my family finally did sit down and figure out what to do with us, their idea was even worse than having us stay at Mom's abandoned house.

I would go and live with my brother Danny, who had been gone since Mom's passing, while Bonita would go off to Carolyn's. I could not believe it. They were splitting up the two closest members of our family. I was sick to my stomach. My emotions were almost completely burned out, and I was barely holding on.

Even though I was brokenhearted to part with Bonita, I really did love the idea of living with Danny. I had always wanted to be just like him. He was the one of us who had gone off to college and gotten himself a nice job. He had a beautiful wife and a great house. In my eyes, Danny had really made it.

Throughout my childhood, I had stayed with Danny's family some weekends and had fun with them. His neighborhood had a community pool with tons of kids I made friends with. He had always made me feel like a welcome addition. The prospect of living with him was a dream come true.

But like most of the dreams I had around that time, it was shattered into a million pieces. At the last minute, Danny backed out without an explanation. Most likely he did not want an interruption to his routine family life. All I knew was that it just did not happen.

I wanted to die. *Did I do something?* I thought. *Is there something wrong with me?* Inside I crumbled and snapped. All those empty promises had taken their toll, and as far as I was concerned everyone could go to hell. I would not be betrayed anymore. I gave up on everyone, and trust was a complete joke.

When Danny didn't take me in, Carolyn did, which meant that Bonita and I stayed together after all. However, now Bonita and I were far apart in mind and spirit. Whereas I had cracked and lost interest in school and pretty much everything, she kept herself together and remained a good student, ensuring a good life to come. Arm in arm, we had faced some serious trials and tribulations, but when it came right down to it, a fork divided our path. She took the high road, and I just wandered aimlessly.

It did not help that I was back in Carolyn's world, which was definitely not the right place for two young teenagers to be. She was a straight-up booster, a hustler who took to the local waterfront where tricks were made, johns were played, and she could've been killed any second. Yeah, Carolyn gave me a roof over my head but no positive guidance. School, in particular, was a disaster.

Toward the final days of eighth grade at Hartman Junior High, I stopped going to school on a regular basis and found myself in danger of failing out. But before I had the chance to be held back due to academics, two other factors assisted in the process: Riley and Ernest Smith.

The Smiths were cousins in my grade and notorious bullies. One day when we were riding home on the bus, they and their friends decided to test me to see what I was made of.

While I sat beside some other random kid near the aisle, just doodling in my notebook, Riley Smith walked up. "Hey, man, move over. You can sit in the middle."

What? This dude wanted me to scoot over like some passive nobody so he could have the aisle seat? He was out of his mind.

"Sorry, man," I said. "This is my seat, and I ain't moving. If you want to sit down, you can take the middle or keep on moving down the line."

Riley did not say a word and made his way to the back of the bus.

That's what I'm talking about, I thought and assumed that was the end of it. I was wrong.

When we pulled up to Riley's stop, he and his cousin Ernest and all their boys jumped me from behind right there in the aisle of the bus. I tried to fight their flurry of punches the best I could, even landing some good shots of my own, but they overwhelmed me in a tight spot with a good ass-kicking.

I was thinking, *Wow! They got me just like that?* I was far more stunned than hurt, trying to digest what had happened. As I sat there, I thought about the fact that none of my boys—Fran, Terry, or Wendell—had done anything to help. *It's worthless to trust anyone*, I thought. *I'll take care of myself.* I knew if I didn't act fast, this would happen again. *This shit ends tomorrow.*

That night as I drifted off to sleep, I imagined myself heroically destroying the Smiths and their gang in front of everyone in a whirlwind of Bruce Lee karate moves. When that fantasy wore off, I knew things would have to be handled a different way. I just wasn't sure how.

The next day while I waited at the bus stop, anxiety swirled in my gut.

Bill, this cool white kid who was my friend, walked up. "I saw what those guys did to you yesterday, man. Take this." He pulled out a nine-inch, pearl-handled buck knife.

My sweaty right hand gripped the knife, and I slipped it into my jacket pocket. When the bus came, I ran on board and waited for the next pickup, which would be the Smiths. As we approached their stop, I looked out the window and was surprised to see Riley all by himself.

That punk got on the bus and immediately talked about kicking my ass the previous day.

That was it. I jumped out of my seat, brandished the blade, and went after Riley. I lunged, trying to stab him.

Ghost white, he tried to fend me off.

I cursed at him and got my digs in. "You gonna fuck with me now, motherfucker? Huh? Now what are you gonna do when I frag your ass right here, right now?"

He shielded himself with schoolbooks and didn't say a word.

The other kids on the bus were going nuts, yelling and screaming. It sounded like a little prison riot. Meanwhile, the bus driver just kept on driving.

Wendell and Terry got up in a panic and tried to grab me, but I was swinging wildly, like a blind man wielding a cane to fight off a robber. With the blade swinging back and forth like a lightning-fast pendulum, my boys backed off too.

Riley wasn't such a tough guy anymore. His eyes welled with tears. Without the assistance of his little gang, he was revealed for all he was: a terrified bully. It was great to finally scare the hell out of him.

I put the knife back in my pocket and punched his left cheek. The shot was so hard I thought my hand was broken as he crashed into the rear emergency exit door.

Proud of myself, I calmly sat down. All the kids, especially Riley, must have thought I was crazy and too dangerous to be messed with. *Mission accomplished*, I mused. Surely word of what had happened would spread like wildfire throughout the school, and I would be granted permanent king-of-the-halls status.

The more I thought about it throughout the school day, however, I realized there was no way in hell Riley would let that humiliating moment merely fade away. In fact, some other kids told me to expect a swift payback the next morning.

The following day, I skipped school and went to the movies. I hoped everything would blow over and I would be good to go by the end of the week.

When I finally did return, the campus security guard immediately grabbed me and took me to the principal's office, where both Riley and Ernest sat. I guess the bus driver had seen more than I'd thought and had gone straight to the office to tell them about the incident.

I looked at the principal, with his pasty face and gray eyes, and told him the whole story, starting with the Smiths and their friends jumping me. "I only brought the knife to defend myself by scaring them off. I'm not going to come to school every day and get beat on by anybody, let alone a whole group of punks like them."

The principal took a good, long stare at me. "Well, it's good you didn't come to school yesterday, because these gentlemen had a surprise for you too." He pulled out a long cane and showed me how the handle could pop off to reveal a short sword just like the one Alex had in *A Clockwork Orange*. It was pretty chilling to imagine what those dudes might have done with it.

Considering how very close we had come to killing each other, the punishment was appropriately severe. We were all suspended for the remaining school year, which meant I was going to have to repeat the eighth grade. Since the last day was only about two months away, I tried to tell myself it was a nice extension to summer vacation.

The chaotic and unpredictable life I was leading after my mother's death was finally catching up with me.

INTO THE FIRE

Even though I didn't have many positive role models in my life, thankfully Carolyn was still seeing Luther, the one who'd taken care of all the arrangements for Mom's funeral. In addition to the funeral parlor, he owned a nightclub, a ranch, and a few other businesses. He was the most successful and honest businessman I'd ever known, and I wanted to be just like him one day.

When Luther was busy running one of his many establishments, sometimes Carolyn would take me to work with her at this tiny little dive bar called the Seashore Lounge, a cool, kick back kind of place at the waterfront. Here I saw a side of life no kid my age had any business encountering.

My sister ran the Seashore's bar, which was a revolving door for pimps, players, and prostitutes doing the daily hustle. Outside the front entrance girls adorned the street, their asses completely hanging out, soliciting any and all who passed by. People were having sex in the bathrooms, behind the Dumpster, and in the backseats of parked cars. They snorted cocaine and shot heroin in plain sight without fear or shame. They were unruly, loud, and free of any worries of the outside world.

For some reason, most likely greased palms, the law turned a blind eye to all the tricking and drug deals going down. The whole scene was like the chaos of the Wild West. Unless someone was stabbed or shot at, the police showed neither hide nor hair. It was just part of an arranged, corrupt understanding as traditional and tried and true as any white-collar contract.

As chaotic as it was, the Seashore was my haven and my rite of passage. Day after day while sweeping the floor or washing dishes, I kept my head down, but my innocent eyes and ears were open. As the wind whipped the scent of salty seawater in, I silently witnessed groups of hookers discussing all the seedy details of their hustles. They howled and shrieked with fits of laughter as they raved over how much money they had taken their clients for. Whether it was in some desperate dude's steamy car or a hasty throw down in the doorway of a closed shop, they were out there giving and taking it any way they could get their claws on it.

"I just took this sucker for a grand," one said, "and I gave it all to my man. I don't keep *anything* from him."

I could not believe the stuff I was hearing. These sad women degraded themselves just to put money in their pimps' pockets.

One thing was for sure. After getting earfuls of this kind of material, I found it nearly impossible to think about going back to school when it reopened in the fall. I was going to be a super duper eighth grader again after being held back. It was frustrating and humiliating, and life was pulling me every which way but to the classroom. How was I supposed to sit there and concentrate on anything when all I was thinking about would have warped the other kids' minds?

The Seashore wasn't the only place I saw people using drugs. They seemed to be everywhere, and it didn't take long for me to encounter them for myself. One day while I was standing at the corner bus stop, this kid I knew named Dominic and his dropout older brother Todd introduced me to the world of weed. Todd pulled out this skinny little joint and sparked it up. I had always wanted to try marijuana, so when Dominic passed the joint over, I took a deep pull from it. A second later I was having a coughing fit, and my eyes were tearing up. Dominic and Todd laughed as I slowly felt the effects for the first time. Yeah, there was no mistaking it: I liked weed. Suffice it to say, I had a new little ritual to look forward to in life.

Marijuana was not the only vice going around. People I knew were doing crazy drugs. It was the late seventies; there seemed to be no laws and no limits. There were Quaaludes, strong sedative pills. There was syrup, which was prescription cough medicine with codeine in it. My sister Billie Jean and Butch, one of her many pimp boyfriends, got pretty inventive and mixed ludes and syrup into a concoction called the Jim Jones Special, in reference to the poisoned Kool-Aid Jim Jones used in the infamous mass suicide at Jonestown. Half a bottle of a Jim Jones Special, and those two would be on their asses and out of their minds for hours. I'd just stare and laugh at their rants and antics. There were also hard drugs, like cocaine and heroin, but I had seen what that crap could do. I had seen strung-out people ruining their lives, and that was a risk I was not interested in.

I definitely liked to hit the weed from time to time, but unless I was out with some of the guys or Carolyn's friends were smoking at the house, I wouldn't be doing it. You would not find me lying around the house smoking joints all day. I was a pretty active young kid, discovering new life lessons at every turn.

Some of those lessons weren't so easy to take. One day at Carolyn's, I barged into a bedroom to find a dude with a belt wrapped around his arm and a needle stuck into it. After the initial shock, I looked into his eyes. It was Luther.

My head spun, and I didn't know which way to turn. I walked out and slammed the door.

How could I have wanted to be like Luther? At a mere fourteen years old, I was lost. If the most successful person I knew was a drug addict, what was the point of following the rules to make a better life for myself? I became even less interested in school. Many weekdays I would ditch class and take the bus to downtown Houston.

One of my favorite escapes was a movie theater called the Majestic Metro. I could pay fifty cents and get lost for hours watching reel after reel, like *Shaft* and *Super Fly*, on the big screen. But the ones that really captured my imagination were

Bruce Lee's kung fu masterpieces, like *Enter the Dragon*. The agility and power of Lee's karate moves mesmerized me. All I could think about was being like him someday and learning his style.

When I did grace the halls of Hartman Junior High, it would be merely for the subjects that interested me. One of those was math, but it wasn't because I had a penchant for fractions and long division. Far from it. My interest was in the teacher, Ms. Hughes. As she wrote out numbers and calculations on the board, the only thing I was taking notes on was her ass. She had that side-to-side shake of a hard-writing teacher, and I was all in.

Ms. Hughes's backside wasn't the only distraction either. I started looking at what was happening in Carolyn's world down at the waterfront and wondered if this would be my fate too. I saw dudes with big cars and fur coats, gold around their necks, and diamonds on their fingers and sometimes envisioned myself in that role too.

It might have been irresponsible for Carolyn to bring me to the waterfront, but I knew she was doing the best she could. I didn't blame her or complain but respected her as my first teacher of the streets. Carolyn had a brazen fearlessness instilled by years of hard living and risk taking. She was also a ruthless woman, and no one wanted to be at odds with her.

Unsuspecting people sometimes crossed that line, though. One night we were all hanging out in the house when we heard a knock at the door. When Bonita looked through the peephole and saw my brother Don, she thought nothing of it. She lifted the burglar bar and let him in.

But behind Don was Clyde, this dope fiend who hung out at the waterfront all the time. He held a gun to my brother's back and pushed his way in.

Panic coursed through my veins.

"Stay the fuck back," Clyde yelled as he waved the gun wildly. Wide-eyed and deranged-looking, he rifled through Carolyn's purse, dresser drawers, cabinets, and whatever else he could get his hands on.

Even though I was scared, an uncontrollable rage filled me. All I wanted to do was get my sister's .38 from her nightstand in the next room. *I want to kill this motherfucker,* I thought repeatedly. Time seemed to stand still, and I felt paralyzed.

Clyde finished ransacking the place, then took Don hostage again and ran out of the house with our belongings.

Carolyn went ballistic. "Where's my gun? That punk-ass junkie thinks he's going to come in my house and pull some shit like that? Ah, hell, no!" She ran into her room, emerged a moment later with her gun, and ran out the front door.

I learned afterward that Clyde had let Don go just down the block, and Clyde had taken off. Freaked out, Don had run off too.

The next day at school, my bizarre balancing act continued as I sat at my desk with the previous night's drama playing in my head. While the kid next to me was probably thinking about what was for lunch or what Archie Bunker had said on last night's episode of *All in the Family*, I was hyped up from being robbed at gunpoint by a lunatic.

Since a stable home life was not in reach, I looked for escape from the stress anywhere and any way I could find it. As much as school didn't interest me, ironically Hartman Junior High provided one of my favorite all-time opportunities: I became drum major with the marching band. The drum major was the equivalent of the leadership role of the quarterback on the football team. It was one of the best times I had during those years.

Within a few weeks, I became adept at my position in the band and gained popularity around the halls. There is no doubt I would not have gone to school at all in those days if it weren't for the band and, of course, Ms. Hughes's ass.

My education outside of school continued to thrive. I still visited Billie all the time to see what was up. At her place in some fleabag motel room, I learned even more. Since there was really nothing for me to do there, she had me babysit some of her pimp boyfriends' kids and things like that while she went out.

Billie was on the streets pulling tricks on dudes, and there I was with the cockroaches being hustled too. The only benefit was the twenty-four-hour marathons of X-rated movies flickering on the television. I had seen debauchery like this in adult magazines at a bookstore once before, when I had been called out by the front counter guy. Now I sat in that motel room warping my brain with garbage for hours.

Those weren't the only lessons I learned at Billie's. One time she asked me to pick up some weed for her and her boyfriend Butch. It wasn't as if I had a choice, and I figured I could get a nice pinch out of the bag for myself along the way.

In an attempt to show off a little for Butch, I said, "Okay, but I want to drive your car to get it."

She shrugged. "Sure, if you think you can handle it."

Hell, yeah, I could handle it.

Butch gave me some cash, I grabbed the keys, and I was out of there for another Booker T adventure.

Wow, this is fuckin' cool, I thought as I raced to the closest hot spot in the area, ran in, and took care of business. Since I knew all the people in the area through Billie, I grabbed the sack without a hitch and made my way back. I was humming along to The Commodores' "Too Hot Ta Trot" on the radio, having a good old time when I saw the cop.

The bag of weed hidden in my pants stunk up the car like a dead skunk. The flashing red and blue lights bounced off all the mirrors and made the interior of the car pop like a silent disco. *Now what?* I sat there sweating.

The cop approached. "Get out of the car, son, and hand it over."

Huh? I got out and acted as dumb as ever, the street code kicking in.

"Give it to me. I've been undercover and saw you come out of that drug house after you parked here for five minutes."

I felt like I was having an out-of-body experience.

"I'm telling you this just one more time, or I'm hauling your ass in. Give me the bag."

Man, I couldn't believe what was happening. The code of lies wasn't working, so I reached into my pants and gave him the sack of weed.

The dude asked me all kinds of questions about the dealers and other cats setting up shop. "We've been running a sting on these places for weeks," he said. "Now give us a name."

No way. It was one thing to give myself up, but to rat out the people of the streets? It was not happening.

Acquaintances milled about, watching the drama unfold.

I was glad to provide the evening's entertainment. "Man, I don't know any of those guys in there. You walk up and put the money in the slot, and then you get your package and leave. You don't know their names or even see their faces."

Stone-faced, the cop stared right through me.

I explained as best I could in a nervous fourteen-year-old, lying-my-ass-off, stuttering voice.

He shook his head and took my name and information. Instead of cuffing and stuffing me, he said, "You're free to go."

How's that? I couldn't believe it. Not wanting to wait for him to change his mind, I turned toward my car to get the hell out of there.

"Oh, you can have this back too." Behind me, the officer held out the bag of weed.

I almost fell over. "For real?"

"Oh yeah, go ahead. You're free."

I know my face must have lit up in utter confusion. I took the bag, slowly turned, and walked away.

"Oh, but of course you know if you leave with that bag, I'll have to arrest you right here and now for possession of marijuana, right?"

I stopped. "Well, then I'll just dump it out and everything's cool, right?"

"No, because if you do that, I'll have to write you up for littering." He smirked. "I guess you'll have to figure out another way to get rid of that bag, won't you?"

Huh? He couldn't have wanted me to smoke joint after joint until it was all gone. "What do you want me to do with it then? Eat it?" I joked.

He wasn't laughing.

Shit. This cop wanted me to consume an entire ounce of dry marijuana. My mind raced. *You've got to be fucking kidding me.* I weighed my options and considered taking the arrest. I stared at the bag, feeling queasy and completely embarrassed. I had never heard of anything like this.

Finally, I decided there was no way around it. It was time for a take-out vegetarian dinner.

I pinched inside that bag of dry seeds and stems and pulled a couple of clusters out. I looked at that cop one more time to see if he was messing around with me. Maybe I could still talk my way out of it.

The look etched on his face said, *Not a chance, kid. Get eating.*

Like a horse with a feedbag around its neck, I slowly took this dirty weed and gagged it all down. I was eating my own new cereal, Booker T's Desert-Dry Sticks and Rocks—*now with extra seeds!* It was completely horrendous and humiliating, but even with the cop and everyone else looking on and laughing, you best believe I swallowed the contents of that whole bag.

Then I walked to my car. The cop never checked if I had a driver's license, which of course I didn't. I drove away free, spitting my guts out and cursing that cop at the top of my lungs.

During the ride of shame back to Billie's, I worried she and Butch would be mad that I had lost their weed due to my unexpected little meal.

To my surprise and relief, they got a kick out of the whole deal. "Boy, go get yourself some ice cream." They chuckled. "You could probably use some dessert about now, right?" More laughter.

What a riot.

They let me off the hook, got themselves a bag from another place, and even let me smoke some to soothe my troubles. All things considered, aside from a sore throat, no real harm had been done.

Most importantly, I was free to see another day and had maintained the integrity of the code by not giving up any names. That cop may have won the battle, but I had helped win the war.

After that, I got to know Butch pretty well, and as I had with so many males who'd drifted in and out of my life, I looked to him as a role model. He was like a big brother to me. When

Billie would take off to the waterfront to take care of business, as she did best, Butch would take me out on excursions. That's when my real classes were in session.

Butch pulled up in his pristine white Cadillac, radio blasting the melodies of Willie Hutch, whose soulful sound of the streets tapped into the pulse of the black community. Butch's favorite nightly routine was to go straight to the waterfront strip to check each of his traps, or the spots where his girls prowled for sex and scored him wads of cash. They were any number of places, not unlike the scenes I heard about at Carolyn's waterfront bar: street corners, sleazebag motels, dilapidated clubs, drug houses, and stoops of abandoned buildings—the kinds of spots where junkies or homeless people would also be looking for handouts or pity.

The hardened and pathetic looks on people's faces, the sound of the seagulls flying overhead, and Butch's condescending commentary all came together like a crooked symphony.

"Look at these fuckin' bums. They make me sick," Butch said. "Don't let that shit happen to you. Stay away from those hard drugs. They'll string your ass out."

Butch, like a fox hunter or a crab fisherman, would check what he had caught in each trap over the last couple of hours. That's when things got really interesting. It was insanely shocking to witness the harsh reality of what happened to these women if they didn't meet their quotas.

With my hands almost covering my eyes, I watched from

the car as he swaggered to them one at a time to have a little chat. If the money was short, there was always trouble. I saw girls smacked sideways, jacked up against brick walls, or beaten to the ground. Butch did not care if it was forty degrees, hailing, or raining. Those girls had to stand out there from dusk till dawn to bring in what was expected.

They never talked back but promised to do better next time. As we would pull away and speed off, I'd see the tears and mascara run down their cheeks.

Butch cursed up a storm. "Dumb bitches better pull it together, or I'll do it for them."

Butch commanded respect, and the threats of what he would do if they didn't pick up the pace were enough to scare the hell out of me. I could only imagine the horror they felt when they saw that white Cadillac and didn't have their dues for the evening.

As perverse as it might sound, I have to admit the shock and awe of what I witnessed made my adrenaline rush. *Whoa, is this what I want to do?* I thought. *Yeah, I think I do.*

I never saw Butch encounter Billie on the strip. I'm sure he avoided that on purpose. Thank God. There's no denying I used to see my sister come home many a night busted up with a bruised cheek or a bloody lip. I never really knew if Butch was responsible, but Billie didn't say a word and I definitely would not ask.

The whole scenario—the waterfront, the rides with Butch, and my sister—was an elaborate learning experience. That's just it: Butch was teaching me. He saw me as a little disciple to be groomed. He always kept me strapped with a little cash of my own so I could feel the part and have a taste to bring me back for more. I think he saw me as himself when he was a kid and liked the idea of having a loyal pupil of the pimp lifestyle to follow in his platform-shoed footsteps.

Back then pimping was a full-time job. Image—character, poise, fashion—was everything. A consistent no-bullshit attitude determined the success of a wheeler and dealer, and Butch was all in. Butch's style was right out of the old blaxploitation movies from the seventies.

Like a method actor, he constantly played the role, his mannerisms deliberate. And man, you should have seen that walk of his. A tried and true pimp limp is as calculated and rhythmic as anything you've ever seen: a slow glide with the left leg followed by a swift kick and thrust with the right. From head to toe and with every action, Butch was a pimping legend and master of the game.

We would go to the barber, and I would sit in the chair next to him listening to his philosophies while he got all groomed for the day. He had his long hair ironed straight with just a little flare of some curls at the end and his long nails meticulously manicured and painted with a high gloss. Meanwhile, I sat there with my chin resting on my hands, watching everything he did.

From my privileged place under Butch's wing, I heard the other pimps in the barbershop exchanging random stories about their girls and talking about the pros and cons of the game. One bragged about having a white chick in his stable. He said of all his girls, she made most of the bread. All these black dudes got a big kick out of the fact that he was selling a white girl's body for his profit. In their eyes, she was white gold.

I felt like Sinbad traveling the Seven Seas listening to salty pirates spinning tales of their conquering voyages. After being trapped in my little tiny comfort zones of Sunnyside and South Park for years under my mom's protective watch, I was experiencing the real world through these pimps' stories. This was far beyond what I had been exposed to while around my sisters. Now I was seeing it from the view of the men in charge of Carolyn's and Billie Jean's worlds.

Watching Butch's showmanship influenced the way I acted at school. Even though I was still barely attending, when I did go I always thought of myself as being like Butch and his pimpin' friends. Thanks to the cash he threw my way, I had the sweetest clothes—the hottest cowboy boots money could buy, designer bell-bottoms with the sharpest creases down the fronts, and entire dresser drawers of short-sleeved IZOD Lacoste shirts with the little crocodile on them. I even had a meticulously sprayed and maintained Jheri curl, which was the highest level of cool at the time. Compared to the other kids in their ratty jeans and untied sneakers, I felt like a man among children.

The other students were like, "Wow, what's he into? Booker's gotta be loaded."

I had flash and balls and sauntered around like I owned the place. It was all a big game to me. I thought, *If I can fake my way through life, why the hell not?*

That's when I considered pursuing Butch's offer to take on his career path. The only part I didn't like and couldn't see myself getting down with was beating the women. I still had nightmares over some of what I had seen. And sometimes I overheard Carolyn talking about some girl found dead in an alleyway or Billie mentioning a girl who never came home again. It was a lot to come to terms with.

As much as I may have fantasized about the grandiose ideas of running the streets like Butch, not once did I take him up on his offer. No matter how hard the dark side was pulling me, deep down I really wanted to do the right thing.

Sure, I saw riches and respect. It was a way of life that had lured in many a lost soul, but I also knew it did not always work out for guys as it had for Butch.

My sister Gayle once had a small-time pimp named Gene. He was a real rags-to-riches brother. Starting with nothing, he set up his business with about four or five girls. Soon he was tricked out with the flashy jewelry and the Cadillac. For quite a while, Gene was a man about town, really making it. The dude was an impressive success. Then out of nowhere, he just kind of disappeared without a trace.

Well, a couple of years later, we were driving around and came up to a red light and there was this guy looking horrible,

78   BOOKER T. HUFFMAN

dressed in rags, propped up on cardboard boxes against the wall. "Hey, man, can I have some money for food?" he said. "I'm cold and starving. Please help me." It was a pathetic sight.

It took me a second to recognize this guy with his overgrown beard and those glazed-over eyes, but the shape of his face and the sound of his voice were clear. It was Gene. This man who had seemed to have it all figured out was curling up for the night in a little shanty made of boxes and garbage.

When I later asked Butch what had happened, he told me Gene had committed the cardinal sin of getting high on his own supply. While making additional money selling drugs, Gene had taken them himself. In the end, the drugs had taken him. Having made a bad choice, he now had to live or die by panhandling on the street. Witnessing the rise and fall of Gene scared me straight out of pursuing the hustling game.

THE ONGOING STRUGGLE

Life was turbulent with Carolyn at the Seashore and with Billie and Butch. I accomplished very little during my second year in eighth grade and the following year in ninth grade. Any ambition for the future became laughable, and my optimism was growing thin. I needed a change of venue, both physically and mentally.

My sister Bonita had graduated from Jesse H. Jones High School the previous spring and had quickly gotten to work. She had a great job at a mortgage brokerage in Dallas and had recently moved into an apartment with her new boyfriend.

I decided to say good-bye to Carolyn for a while and move in with my aunt Vallia Huff, who lived near our old house in South Park. Living with the Huffs seemed like the perfect alternative at the time. Vallia wasn't really my aunt but was the sister of my old stepfather, Robert Hill (yes, the television thief).

Vallia was married to a great guy named Isaac Huff. She was also my boy Fran's mother, which made the whole arrangement extremely comfortable. I had always thought of the Huffs as my own family. It almost felt like I was coming home.

To me, the Huffs had the perfect life. They got along like a real family should, had a great house and a nice car, and most importantly made me a part of it all. They took me in, fed me, and supported my new academic goals.

Although the Huffs lived in South Park in the Jesse H. Jones school district, where Lash and Bonita had gone, I wanted to go to another school. Jack Yates Senior High School, located in the neighboring suburbs of Third Ward, had the best reputation for basketball, football, and my main interest—the band. I decided to get all the necessary registration papers and did what any enterprising and creative sixteen-year-old in my position would do: I lied about my address.

Those were the days when you could manipulate the system without much difficulty. Unfortunately for me, after getting into Yates and making a beeline for the sign-up sheet for the band to settle back into the role of drum major, I was hit with some devastating news. Unlike my previous walk-on experience, the method of operations at Yates was much different. Apparently, a prospective drum major had to earn the role, like a varsity spot on the football team. I was informed that process could take around two years.

Damn. Two years? I thought. Patience had never been one of my virtues. I was not interested in waiting around, so I gave up that idea. As I had during my junior high years, I aimlessly wandered the halls of Jack Yates and picked and chose which classes, if any, to attend.

At the Huffs' house, too, I had one foot out the door. At first I had been completely invested, thinking, *Man, I've never had a family life like this.* But the fact that we weren't true family sometimes bothered me. I could not completely accept the Huffs in my heart. At night in bed, I stared at the ceiling feeling depressed and alone. *This isn't my father. This isn't my family or my lifestyle.* The Huffs were this bonded, regular family, void of the drama of my sisters' comings and goings. These people had meals together and spoke about each other's days and things of that nature. It was alien to me.

I had thought these kinds of interpersonal dynamics only occurred in television shows like *The Brady Bunch* or something. But this was commonplace in the Huff household, and it left me feeling at odds and uncomfortable. The black cloud that had formed when Bonita and I had been left alone in that vacant house still stormed inside me. Nothing in the Huffs' home was really mine, and I developed an abiding feeling that it would all go away at any moment. I prayed everything would just remain as it was, but the fear of abandonment was always there.

Meanwhile, the world of street hustling echoed in my thoughts and at times was a huge distraction. The Huffs were oblivious to the things I had seen and been a part of, and that was probably for the best.

Products of our different environments, Fran and I were at opposite ends of the spectrum. While he was studying and preparing for college, I was dreaming of making fast money. Hearing about my escapades was the last thing Fran needed while he geared up for his next chemistry class or English exam.

Although I was torn between two worlds, I did my best to stay on the straight and narrow. I mean, sure, I had thoughts of pimping out girls and making wads of dough, but I didn't form an actual plan for doing it. Instead, in 1981 when I was sixteen, I got into the huge scene of choreographed street dancing known as pop locking. I'd been a longtime fan of the TV show *Soul Train* with Don Cornelius, and I could not get enough of the cool, synchronized moves they were doing. The music had such a rhythmic flow that there was no resisting the urge to get up and dance.

Years before, in the midseventies, I had seen a group called The Lockers. They were amazing and totally grabbed my imagination. The seven of them had matching costumes, and their rapid-fire and fluid jumps, twists, splits, kicks, and hat flips became a huge sensation. Two of them would go on to even bigger fame. Fred Berry became the memorable character of Rerun on ABC's *What's Happening!!* and Toni Basil went on to sing "Mickey," the number-one pop hit in 1982.

Inspired, I was more than ready to assemble my own group. Along with three others, I formed The Remote Controls and performed not only in Battle Out contests on the streets with other kids but also at our high school talent shows. I choreographed all the routines to songs by artists like Kraftwerk, Soul Sonic Force, and Herbie Hancock. We even wore matching silver vinyl and rubber outfits. (They were actually those jogging suits designed to induce heavy sweating for weight loss.) For the talent shows, we cut the house lights and put on a strobe for maximum effect. We blew the kids in the auditorium away.

The time I had spent as junior high drum major contributed to the success I enjoyed with The Remote Controls. That role had taught me rhythm, style, and grace in performance, which translated perfectly into some of the many exciting moves in my pop locking repertoire.

Now that I had a new outlet of expression, my disappointment over no longer being a drum major was gone. I was feeling confident like never before and enjoying girls' attention. One in particular had my attention too.

Angela was a cute, light-skinned black girl who was an eighth grader at Hartman Junior High, where we'd taken notice of each other the previous year. It hadn't taken long for us to begin passing notes in the halls and start hanging out on occasion, although we never dated each other exclusively.

As my first year at Yates was ending, Hartman was having its last dance before summer vacation and I was definitely going. Sure, I didn't even go there anymore, but everyone crashed dances at all the area schools back then. I remember being at the dance and making the rounds seeing what was up with acquaintances, including Angela of course. The funny thing is that while I was keeping my eyes on her, others at the dance were doing the same and took notice of me.

"Hey, motherfucker, what are you doing here?"

The words came from behind me, but I recognized Riley Smith's voice. Before I even had time to turn, Riley, Ernest, and a couple of other dudes surrounded me. I hadn't seen them since our eighth grade suspension two years before, but I knew things were picking up where they had left off. Suddenly I was in a hard shoving match with Riley, spilling through the crowd to the doors leading outside. Since it was a warm spring night, the dance had an outdoor section too. Just as we found ourselves out near the gate to the parking lot, things escalated.

I threw a punch and cracked Riley square in the jaw, but that didn't stop the others from swarming and overpowering me with fists and kicks. They even threw me over the gate onto the pavement of the parking lot. I landed hard on my ass and elbows.

As I was trying to stand up and gain my composure, the campus security guard ran up and tried to separate all of us. We all hightailed it out of there in different directions. After making it a few blocks away, I looked down at myself. My shirt was all torn up, my tie was muddied, and my elbows were skinned.

"Those motherfuckers," I mumbled as I walked home.

I'll get those assholes. The thought was recurring.

In the end, though, I never saw the Smiths again.

Angela and I entered an on and off relationship. By the time she was about fifteen and I was seventeen, we'd been sexually active together for a while. Back then, at our houses, privacy was always desired but never guaranteed.

One day after school, the Huffs were out and the two of us were alone. We decided to run to Vallia's nice, big, king-size bed. We went to town in it.

On our fourth or fifth session, wouldn't you know it? The door swung open, and there was Aunt Vallia, shocked as hell to see us there. She turned and stormed out, not saying a word. She didn't need to.

Angela jumped up, grabbed her clothes, and ran into the bathroom.

I rolled over, put my clothes on, and went to do some damage control with Vallia.

To my surprise, she did not say much. "Don't ever let me catch you doing that shit in my bed again, okay?"

It was a reasonable request. I agreed, and then we had a laugh about it. Aunt Vallia was one cool lady.

Unfortunately, that was when and where all existing fun with Angela ended permanently.

A few weeks later, Angela's grandmother called and asked me to come to her house. Anxiety filled my stomach. *This can't be good*, I thought. *I hope this isn't what I think it is.* I walked upstairs to ask Fran for a ride.

As I rode the few miles to Angela's house, Fran sat in the driver's seat, prodding me a little over the situation and trying to joke around. I was in no mood. I stared out the passenger window, watching the trees go by and the pale sunlight flickering through the branches behind. It was a drive I had ridden a hundred times before, but this was far different. My mind raced as we turned onto Belford and crossed over the railroad tracks.

When we finally pulled up, I felt like a death row inmate about to walk a long corridor toward the electric chair.

Fran shook my hand, leaving me with some words of encouragement. "Hey, man, better you than me." He laughed.

I flashed him a wide-eyed look of death. "Real fuckin' funny." I slammed the door and marched up the front walk.

The door opened. "Booker, she's pregnant." Angela's grandmother lowered the axe. Standing about five foot three inches tall, the heavyset woman glared at me, the whites of her eyes contrasting with her dark skin.

"Huh?" Although it was exactly the news I had been afraid of, it was baffling.

Angela was not even there. I knew she had already been given the business, and now it was my turn.

"So," she said, "what do you intend to do? You need to consider doing the right thing and marrying Angela. You've got to bring this child into the world the right way."

Whoa. This lady was going straight for the jugular. *Marriage? Baby? Not a chance. Not me, not now.* I scrambled for answers and excuses. "But I don't have a job," I muttered.

"Get one."

Damn. I was sweating. There was no way I was marrying

Angela. In fact, I was not even convinced the baby was mine. We had both been seeing other people. I felt like I was being cornered into something that was not my responsibility. Besides that, I was not ready for it. I still had many years of independence and partying to experience before fatherhood.

With the issues I had rolling around in my head over the early deaths of my own parents and my unstable life with my siblings, the concept of parenthood was way too much for me.

"I have to go," I said and literally ran out of there.

Afterward, I stopped speaking to Angela and never called her. If she tried to reach me, I simply didn't take the calls. I just hoped she would get the picture and go away. I wanted as much distance from her as possible.

When it came time for school to start back up, I decided not to go. Over the course of my next year, if I actually did show up, it was just to hang out and get into trouble. I faced the fact that Booker T. Huffman was not cut out for academics, so why continue to waste time?

I made the choice to quit and felt a freedom I never had before. Gone was the nagging sense that I always had to be a part of that system. I felt like a thousand-pound weight had suddenly been lifted from my shoulders, and it was amazing.

That was it for my scholastic career. Even though I was the only one in my family who did not finish school, it didn't bother me in the slightest. I felt like a man, doing my own thing with no one to answer to. I was the master of my own destiny. The possibilities seemed endless.

However, I wasn't sure what I was going to do. I was seventeen, broke, and had no prospects. My newfound freedom led to an all-time low. For the first time in my life, I decided to find a legitimate job. I looked around for a week or two and found myself working at a Fiesta Mart in South Park, hating every second of it.

Fiesta Mart was one of those one-stop-shop kind of places like Walmart or Target. It stocked clothes, boots, records, tapes, and every type of food product imaginable. As usual, it did not take me long to get some ideas. I was doing all the mundane tasks—stocking shelves, bagging groceries—and I was also stealing.

Believing I could get away with anything, I walked out in a brand-new pair of cowboy boots one day. Another time, it was some sneakers. Then I would have a steak tucked under my shirt. Within a few weeks on the job, my closet at Vallia's looked like a cross between Cowtown Boots and Foot Locker, and the Huffs' refrigerator looked like the meat locker at a Sizzler steak house. It was great.

Best of all, the theft kept my street credibility intact even while I worked such a lame job. I felt like a grocery store mastermind giving the proverbial middle finger to the store security at every turn. It was open season in that place for a young criminal like me, and I had myself a field day. Free was free—and if it was free, it was for Booker T.

One day I just did not want to go to work. I preferred to sit around and smoke, so I called up the manager.

In a lame attempt at a high-pitched woman's voice, I said, "Yes, hello, Mr. Napier? This is Billie Jean Huffman, Booker's sister. I'm calling on his behalf because he's not feeling well today and won't be able to make it in. Have a good day, sir."

"Well, then you tell Booker when he's feeling better he can come in and pick up his last check. He's fired."

I was so rattled that I almost lost it and went back to my regular voice, but I stayed in character and stammered something incoherent before the dial tone interrupted me.

What? Damn, I thought. *I just got shit-canned for impersonating a woman.* I was so embarrassed.

With my head down, I quickly crept into Fiesta Mart to pick up that check. As soon as I had grabbed it, I rushed out of there, kissing my grocery store career good-bye.

My fledgling career in the retail industry was over, and I was still living on Vallia's goodwill. I thought more and more about earning something of my own instead of relying on others. Having dropped out of school and knowing Angela was out there pregnant brought me to a personal crossroads. I thought of the old hustle game I'd seen at Carolyn's and Billie's. I decided to reconnect and see if I had other options.

I called Carolyn, who had moved into a house in the north side of town, and asked if I could stay with her yet again. It felt like some weird, unnecessary game of ghetto musical chairs or something. She said I could, and I started mentally preparing for yet another unknown venture in my confused life.

During dinner with Vallia, Isaac, and Fran, I explained my decision to move to Carolyn's. I could tell by Vallia's reaction that it was a welcome idea. I am sure my unpredictable lifestyle, Angela's pregnancy, my obvious drug use, and my being fired from Fiesta were too much for her. Besides, she and Isaac clearly would not want Fran to take any cues from me. I loved the Huffs for taking me in, and I would never forget the love and the roof they had given me, yet for all our sakes it was time to part ways.

Now that I was a seasoned man of nearly eighteen, I was more aware of the steady stream of weird dudes coming in and out of the house to see Carolyn. She had many friends with benefits, who no doubt helped take care of her financially.

In a foolhardy move, I decided to confront my sister about it. "Why are all these guys constantly coming in here? They're just taking up space and it's getting annoying."

Big mistake.

Carolyn went ballistic on me, saying that what she did was none of my business. We went back and forth pretty hard, and it was really ugly. Finally, she cut loose and shouted, "Junior, pack up all your shit and get out of my house. I don't care what you have to do or where you go, but get the fuck out."

I was devastated. I sat against the curb with my stuff in garbage bags, racking my brain for a solution. Here I was, completely abandoned all over again. Panic set in as I weighed my options. I did not want to go back to the craziness of Billie's. I could not crawl back to Aunt Vallia's. Bonita was in Dallas. Only one conceivable solution surfaced: Lash.

Lash and I had been pretty disconnected for the last four years. Since he had left Bonita and me at our abandoned house to stay with his friend, we had not spent much quality time together. Other than my few visits, we had gone to some local professional wrestling matches, but that was about it.

Beyond desperate, I called my brother and told him what had happened.

To my surprise, he said, "You can stay at my apartment for a while. We'll figure it out."

During such a dark and hopeless moment in my life, his invitation filled my heart with much-needed encouragement.

In the last few years, Lash had been doing respectably well for himself. He had a place of his own in southeast Houston and a pest control job. During his work hours, he drove around in a truck designed to look like a mouse, complete with giant ears attached to the roof and a little tail hanging from the rear doors. I almost fell over laughing when I saw it, but I held it in. I mean, at least he had a job and was supporting himself, which was way more than I could say for myself.

Lash was living in a place called Willow Creek Apartments. Moving in with him after all that time was interesting, to say the least. We might have been brothers, but we were in completely different frames of mind. We did not see eye to eye on much of anything, but for some reason we both loved boxing and could always have a blast watching the fights on television. Otherwise, we struggled to find common ground.

One difference I saw in Lash after not having visited him for a while was how big he'd gotten. His chest and arms were thick, and he was almost six foot five. For whatever reason, whether his size, his Chevy El Camino or his charming personality, the dude always had girlfriends coming and going. All I knew was that I wanted what he had.

Thankfully, he was willing to help me work out. He started me at the apartment just doing things like push-ups and crunches. I was sore as hell after each workout, but after a few weeks I saw a real difference in my body. I was hooked. When Lash saw I had been sticking with it and was working hard, he brought me to the gym to take it to the next level.

Lash was also serious about making me earn my way. "If you want to stay here with me for a while longer, you need to find a job and chip in."

Yeah, that was fair, so I looked around. Before I knew it, I was flipping burgers and serving one Frosty after another at

Wendy's. Since it was only about a mile and a half from the apartment, I could walk to work. It may have been slightly demoralizing to wear the little red shirt and black cap, but to tell you the truth, working fast food was not that bad at all. Things were really looking up for me.

7

A SON IS BORN

I went to work at Wendy's every day and followed it up with a trip to the gym. Going to work out all the time also helped me break a nasty habit I had recently picked up. Over the last couple of years while I'd spent time with Carolyn and Billie Jean, they were always smoking cigarettes. It hadn't been long till I was bumming one here and there and eventually finding myself with a pack at all times. Now that I was working out, I was smoking right up to the gym door as I walked in and then lighting up as soon as I was finished. The strain on my body was becoming apparent.

One day after nearly coughing up a lung after a set on the bench, I had a moment of realization. *What the hell am I doing smoking these things? I'm trying to improve myself, not go downhill.* That was all it took. I went outside, grabbed my full pack of cigarettes, crushed it, and quit cold turkey just like that.

My confidence as a strong-willed young man grew by the day. For the first time it felt like I was building the foundation of my own life brick by brick. It had started with working out, then had increased when I'd gotten the Wendy's gig to pay rent to Lash, and now I was making healthy choices. I was convinced that if things continued the way they were going, I could be somebody. And that was something I had never imagined before.

It's not like I thought there was a long-term future for me at Wendy's or anything, especially without a diploma, but there was just the persistent feeling that I was on the right path for once. After all those years without my big brother around, his positive influence was there for me when I needed it most.

Now that I had some extra spending money in my pocket, Lash took me out to the clubs at night and I got to see him in action as he did some DJ work. Every door to every club opened when he came rolling up.

I thought, *Man, look at him go! My brother's the shit.* I watched with wonder as he smoothly navigated from table to table and person to person like a slick diplomat. He had ladies hugging on him, and he shook hands with every dude who walked up to him. Everyone seemed to gravitate toward him. The response was electric. Now more than ever, I wanted to be like my big brother. I knew deep down that if Lash could achieve such a cool life, I could too. He was a positive role model who motivated me to keep pushing on to something better.

Now working out took center stage of my priorities. After just a few months banging out the weights at the gym with Lash, I went from 165 to 195 pounds, and it felt great.

Lash was excited about our little training duo and came in one day with two matching leather weight belts. "I've got a great idea." He beamed. "We'll be like a rasslin' tag team. Check these out."

The back of my belt said Mr. Ebony II. Of course, his said Mr. Ebony I. As little kids, we had watched a masked black wrestler named Mr. Ebony on the local *Houston Wrestling* show. Of course, this would be our homage to him. It was a real kick.

Lash had always wanted to be a professional wrestler and constantly said we should give it a try someday. I guess to him the belts made that goal seem one step closer. We would come in with our matching weight belts, and people would stare, trying to figure it out. It was great. The extra motivation helped us both make great gains in the gym.

I had grown over the last year or so, reaching around six foot one, and now it seemed my body was reaching a pinnacle. I instinctively knew that somehow all this training was going to be a ticket out of this common life and into something special. It was just a matter of time and self-discovery.

I began training with one of Lash's best friends Darryl Bates. Much like Lash, he was an inspiration. He worked for the local fire department and had this amazing physique, with biceps that just burst out of his sleeves and screamed strength. He also had a really hot girlfriend and a new car. Darryl seemed to have everyone's respect for all the right reasons. Man, to me, it just did not get any better than that. What more could a person want?

While Lash was the one who first took me to the gym, Darryl taught me how to train at another level. He showed me all his techniques and how to use different machines to develop a routine that would optimize every workout. He was like another big brother.

I was so completely happy to have these positively charged people around me. I had a new brotherhood, a family that protected me and had my best interests at heart. My self-confidence skyrocketed, and I took pride in the hard work I was putting in at the gym. I even made sure my Wendy's shirt was pressed so I could roll up the sleeves and show off my developing biceps. Although it might have been somewhat ridiculous to display my fledgling muscles, it sure seemed to work. Girls everywhere were taking notice.

One in particular also lived in Willow Creek Apartments. Her name was Michelle, and we started seeing each other on a regular basis. Things progressed so quickly between us that she asked me to move in with her. It was a big prospect for a young guy like me, especially considering the fact that Michelle was white and came from an affluent family.

It was an interesting experience, to say the least, the day she decided to take me to meet her parents at their home, which looked more like the White House, in the upper-class Houston suburb of Clear Lake.

"Mom, Daddy, I want you to meet Booker," she said with a smile. "We've been dating for a little while now."

"Oh, so nice to meet you, Booker," her father said as he casually glanced at Michelle and then his wife.

Sure, her parents were nice enough, so cordial and polite, but I could sense the cardiac arrest erupting in both of their chests.

Looking back now, I know Michelle was parading me around to shove the king daddy of all rebellion in her parents' faces. At the time, though, I was just happy to be there. All smiles, I put my best foot forward and tried to be a gentleman.

I have to admit there was something elitist about dating Michelle. I had this rich white girl as arm candy, and a touch of what I'll call trophy syndrome came over me. If all that sounds sort of snobbish, that's probably because it was. Hey, life is life, and I was trying to elevate myself from the deflated existence I'd experienced for way too long. If going out with a white chick made me feel better about myself, a white chick it was gonna be. It sure beat the insufferable drudgery I had been crawling through just months before.

With all that in mind, it was an easy decision to move in with her at Willow Creek. I'm not going to say I was in love with her, but we were definitely in a serious relationship. We were committed to each other and did everything together, like getting ice cream or going to the movies, and it felt good. It felt right.

Up until then, I had never experienced a relationship with a girl at that level. We shared everything, listened to each other's problems, and were completely there for one another. I was really enjoying the intimacy and trust Michelle and I had.

However, by no means were we free of the usual drawbacks of a relationship. We had our rocky moments, as every couple does, but we were mature enough to move past the petty, trivial arguments. But occasionally another issue beyond our control reared its ugly head.

One time we went for a little lovers' stroll in the nearby park, holding hands, minding our own business. As we enjoyed the day and took in the sights, someone in the distance pierced the peace with a scream.

"Nigger lover!"

Michelle and I looked at each other quizzically. Obviously, hearing something like that took me aback. Having never been in an interracial relationship before, I hadn't anticipated being on the receiving end of that kind of hate speech.

I suppose it was to be expected. Racism was just one of those old stigmas that wasn't ever going away. Sometimes we would hear comments in a crowd, or someone would mumble something. I never got into a fight with anyone over it. I knew the people who would make those remarks were cowards, because nobody would ever dare say them directly to our faces.

I felt horrible for Michelle, though. If it weren't for me, she wouldn't have been subjected to any of that unnecessary tension. It's hard enough to make a relationship work as it is, but when undeserved fuel is dumped onto a fire, it can be frustrating.

However, we let those things roll right off our backs and never even really acknowledged them. The greatest downfall between Michelle and me didn't have anything to do with race at all. It was something much simpler and far more gut-wrenching.

At Willow Creek we had a basketball court where I used to shoot around. After going a few times, I met this cool dude named Melvin, who I called Mel, and we played one-on-one and pickup games. We got along great, and like any friends do, we talked about everything—our jobs, things we wanted to do with our lives, and of course girls.

One time after a game, Mel was kicking it about this chick he'd recently started seeing. He told me the graphic play-by-play of all the sexual exploits they were up to.

I listened with a big smile, and then I talked the same game about Michelle and me, except that I never mentioned her by name.

Man, we laughed our asses off at the deviance both of us got into with our chicks.

Then he said his girl's name was Michelle.

I stopped dead in my tracks. "What's her last name?"

He told me.

It was *my* Michelle. I was completely crushed. "Yo, Mel, I *live* with Michelle. That's my girl."

Mel's face dropped, and he went dead silent for a minute, obviously not knowing what to say. He just looked at me stunned and tried to apologize.

I didn't want to hear it. I left the court quickly, telling him, "Don't worry about it." It wasn't his fault anyway, and I didn't hold it against him. He had no idea she was dating someone else.

Stomach turning, head spinning, wondering what had just happened to my seemingly perfect life, I stormed back to the apartment. All of a sudden, everything I had held so close to my heart had turned against me. I had never experienced such betrayal and emotional devastation at the hands of a girl. Not only was she cheating on me, but she was doing it right under my own nose in the same complex. It was beyond anything I had ever anticipated, and the hurt was overwhelming. It had never occurred to me that a woman would be so devious and backhanded, and I felt like a moron for being so oblivious. My blood was boiling, and all I could think about was getting even.

After I confronted Michelle about Mel, she broke down crying and admitted everything. She apologized repeatedly, begging me to stay.

That's exactly what I did. I stayed. But my motivation wasn't reconciliation. Sure, I still had emotional investment in this girl, but the truth of the matter was that my street mentality had kicked in and I was obsessed with getting revenge.

First I convinced her to sign over the apartment lease in my name. She was so desperate to do anything I asked that it didn't take any effort. I just gave her a pen and a stare and said, "If you want me to stay and feel like our relationship is important to you again, you have to show me by putting me on the lease."

She bought it and went all the way with the paperwork, making me the primary on the agreement. I now had full legal control of the place.

With the lease out of the way, I had her also sign a waiver stating that I owned all the furniture in the apartment. She had some really nice property in there. I was putting my chess pieces in such great positions that Bobby Fischer would have pulled out his paper and pen to take notes.

Despite my anger, for a while I truly did try to make it work with Michelle. But it was impossible. Every time we argued about anything, it went right back to Mel. Her cheating proved to be a fatal strike to what we'd once had.

Our fighting escalated out of control until one time she came at me and tried to throw a punch. I quickly pushed her hands out of the way. She ran to call the cops.

When the police showed up, she spun ridiculous lies to try to get me arrested. "He was grabbing me and tried to choke me."

I stood there listening and looking at the cops, thinking, *Ah, shit, here we go. They're gonna take me to jail.*

They probably would have had I not known one of them from the club scene with Lash. He didn't buy her story, but he did pull me aside and warn me. "Book, you better watch out for this kind of shit. You can land in jail real easy when a woman makes claims like what she's saying."

I told him I understood and thanked him for giving me a break, and they took off.

Michelle's attempt to incriminate me that night was the last straw. Because she had signed the apartment and everything over to me, I kicked her out of her own place. I kept it all—the bed, the couches, the television, and even the phone she had used to call the cops on me. In my mind, I had to get her back for what she had done. She'd gotten in way over her head. Checkmate.

After the breakup, my old downward spiral started again. Without the stability and influence of Michelle and being all alone in the apartment, I was tempted to revert to old street behaviors. For the time being, I put my blinders on and remained focused.

On December 29, 1983, Angela gave birth to my son, Brandon T. Huffman. Although I'd had my doubts that I was his father, I accepted that he was my own. But man, Brandon couldn't have come into a more turbulent time. Angela and I had not really spoken much at all since her grandmother had cornered me about nine months earlier. As I had with Angela, I initially did the wrong thing and ignored Brandon as well. I just could not face the gravity of it all.

When Angela called up on occasion and asked for money to help out, I did not give her a dime. I refused to even see my new son. I simply could not let go of my resentment toward her. In the balance, Brandon suffered from the lack of a father's support.

After a few more weeks passed and I really thought about my behavior as a man toward this baby, I began to feel differently. I can't explain it exactly, but some instinctual click went off inside of me. I could not get Brandon off my mind. I knew I had to at least try to do right by this little boy. No matter how selfish I was, the only choice that made sense was to give fatherhood the best attempt possible with my limited resources.

For the sake of our son, Angela and I reconciled enough to manage a fair arrangement for Brandon. It worked at first, but then Angela began playing ridiculous head games with me, putting unnecessary stipulations on my visits with my boy. For example, she would not let me have Brandon if she knew I would be with another woman at the same time, which made no sense to me. I thought without a doubt she was bitter because I had not married her and we didn't have that picture-perfect family.

I didn't know what she was thinking by using our son as a tool to exact her revenge on me, but her plan was backfiring. I never reacted well to being told what to do. Anyone who knew me could have predicted my response. "If you don't want me to see him, I won't," I said. "That's on you."

Still there were times she compromised and brought Brandon over and let me have him for the weekend. It was great. Brandon was such an adorable baby, and I just sat and stared at him as he slept in my arms. It was a powerful feeling to have such a tiny and helpless piece of my own flesh and blood cradled on my chest. That special bond was forming between father and son, and I imagined how close we would be for the rest of our lives.

The heartbreaking truth of it all is that due to Angela's growing frustration over my rejection of her, the pressure of being a single mom, and whatever else might have been going on in her life, she eventually spun out of control. In a short span of time, Angela began hanging out with a bad crowd and developed a newfound penchant for heavy drug use, which affected her ability to care for Brandon. In fact, she stopped caring about him completely, and her grandmother was unwilling to take on the responsibility.

I simply could not handle it all. Without a good-bye, I cut off communication with Angela again. Not a day went by that I didn't think of how Brandon was doing, and my heart grew unbearably heavy. Brandon was now abandoned emotionally just as I had been all those times in my earlier days. It was a bad call but the only one I could come up with.

After Brandon was out of my life and I no longer had Angela intruding in my business, things resumed to normal. I was still working at Wendy's, trying to assimilate and create some semblance of a decent existence. By now it was the spring of 1984, and I was nineteen and still wondering where things would go for me. Although I had done a good job of staying out of trouble and minding my own business, sometimes turmoil would just seem to find me.

In the beginning of my days at Wendy's, I had walked to work because it was so close. But now I had been transferred to another location a few more miles away and had to use the bus system. After the second bus dropped me off in town, I had to wait almost thirty minutes for the third.

After everything I had been through over the years, I was always leery about being in town alone. I always carried nunchakus in a little satchel and was pretty damn good with them. They were my equalizer. *In case of emergency, break glass, grab nunchakus, kick some fuckin' ass.*

One day while I was waiting on the sidewalk for the bus to

arrive, I overheard this guy next to me talking to another dude. Even though I was listening to music on my headphones, the volume was low enough for me to hear everything he was saying.

"I need to get my hands on some fuckin' money real bad, man."

I glanced at him. He looked ragged and strung out. My first thought was, *I'll bet the farm he's fiending for some coke or heroin.*

He didn't pay much attention to me, maybe because of my headphones. He was getting really agitated and pacing manically, gripping something in his front jacket pocket. I assumed he had a knife and didn't want to find out. After listening to this guy's rants, I wondered when this derelict would do something.

A businessman with a briefcase crossed the street to catch a different bus. This desperate crackhead followed, picking up his pace to catch up to the unsuspecting guy strolling through the intersection. Just when the junkie was within ten feet of striking distance, the bus roared up, opened the doors, and the man made it in, completely oblivious to how close he had come to serious harm.

As the bus took off, the druggie stood there looking defeated. Then he stormed back to my area and began loudly ranting to his buddy. "I was that close. Did you see that shit? Fuck!"

I couldn't stand the unpredictability and tension, so I ducked into a nearby game room to wait it out. The last thing I needed was for this dude to start something with me and ruin the decent progress I'd been making in life.

After waiting for about five minutes, I noticed a big crowd

gathering outside the game room window. I walked out and pushed my way through the people to see what the commotion was about. A man lay on the ground with blood squirting out of his heart with each pulse.

It was the most horrifying thing I had ever seen. It turned out my feeling about that junkie had been right on. He had robbed and stabbed some poor guy and left him for dead. I stood there in complete confusion, just taking it all in.

No one could do anything for the man as he was going into shock, terror on his face.

In the midst of all this, my bus pulled up. I got in and sat down, looking at the dying man on the ground as we drove away. I kept thinking, *That could've been me.*

All day at work I told the story to anyone who would listen. Venting what I'd seen helped me process the imagery pounding in my mind. Another one of life's lessons had been thrown in my face, reminding me how randomly tragedy could strike.

THE WENDY'S BANDITS

The traumatic memory of the sidewalk stabbing remained at the forefront of my thoughts for days. Meanwhile, the drudgery of Wendy's was getting me down. Working the same dead-end job every day for hours on end with no hope of advancement played games with my head. It got to the point that I couldn't stand looking at my coworkers. At home I saw those popular "Where's the beef?" commercials on television and lost it. All I could think about was punching that old lady to show her exactly where the damn beef was. It was driving me crazy, and I didn't know how much longer I could hack it.

I was so relieved when a friend from Willow Creek Apartments came on board to help relieve the monotony. I'd met Zach and his wife around the pool, and he and I had played basketball here and there. The minute I first saw him, I could tell he was from the streets, and I gravitated to him. In fact, Zach had been in prison for robbery. Although he had a definite edge, he carried himself with a cool, laid-back attitude that was a welcome addition at work.

Before I knew it, my twentieth birthday had come and gone, but I was still really impressionable and open to all kinds of ideas. One of my brilliant new schemes came after I reunited with Billie Jean, who was now living nearby and running with a new pimp named Toffa.

Toffa lived in an apartment adjacent to Billie's and was a stereotypical Rastafarian, complete with long, thick, ropelike dreadlocks. His accent was so thick it was almost impossible to understand a word he said. He was also one of the major marijuana dealers in Houston. I had never seen anything like his weed business before. Sure, over the years I had seen some operations here and there, but what I walked into this time was some serious action.

Once Toffa got to know me and felt I could be trusted, he decided to show me what was going on in an additional apartment he rented across the courtyard. When I walked in, my jaw almost hit the floor. The first thing I saw was a table with at least ten pounds of marijuana in a huge pile on top.

"Holy shit," I said, unable to stop staring like it was the first naked girl I'd ever seen. "That's a lot of weed."

Toffa stood there smiling like a proud father.

Sitting all around the table were a bunch of people just cutting and chopping away, preparing the weed for plastic bags. Smoke was everywhere. I could barely even see my hands. My mind was doing backflips as I kept trying to process the scene.

Hanging out with Billie and Toffa became paramount among my weekly responsibilities. It was hard to say no to an endless supply of sweet, stinky weed that seemed to whisper in my ear day and night: *Pssst, hey, Booker, wanna get high again?* Hell, yes, I did.

Billie made me an offer. "Toffa and I want to put you down. You interested?" Putting me down, or setting me up with a side job of selling weed, was her way of helping me. She said, "Listen here. Fast money goes fast, and you have to stay on top of the game or it will pass you by. So are you in or out?"

That's exactly how things went with my sister. Billie was by no means a dummy. She had graduated high school and had some book smarts for sure, but her methods of operation after her senior year were not based on a classroom education by any means. She had earned her degree from the streets, magna cum laude. My sister was the type who would see a less-than-practical opportunity and say, "This is probably a bad idea, but fuck it, let's do it anyway." And she would.

My mother always told me, "Junior, you know right from wrong. There's no gray area." However, Billie had made her own rule book: *The World Is Nothing but Gray Area.* I decided to follow her lead and started working for Toffa selling weed. I slung five- and ten-dollar bags all day, but I usually smoked more than I sold.

Eventually Toffa decided to cut his losses and fired me. We all had a good laugh at how terrible I was while we smoked some more.

Of course, I never mentioned any of this weed business to Lash. My brother had been against drugs since I could remember. Lash and I hadn't seen each other much anyway.

I did bring my boy Zach around, though. We used to smoke together and laugh about Wendy's and the people we worked with. We both especially hated the manager.

Zach was one of those people who influenced my mentality—and probably not for the best. I was sick and tired of the monotony in my life and was looking for a means to mix things up a little. Zach turned out to be just what I was seeking.

We developed a little crew of our own with Fran, Wendell, and Terry, and our clique became inseparable. We did everything together. Zach and I could not wait for the minutes to count down on the clock at Wendy's. We would get out of there to meet up with the others and hit the club scene. We were populating the local circuit so often that everyone knew not to mess with any of us, because the rest were sure to be close behind. We became a force to be reckoned with, and it felt great to be a part of something so strong and secure.

We became the most important thing in our lives. We had each other's backs at all times. For unity and flash, we wore matching Adidas warm-up suits with our new nicknames stitched across the backs. Mine was Nature Boy in honor of professional wrestler "Nature Boy" Ric Flair. Zach's was Z-Boy. Wendell's was

Mr. Big Stuff, and Fran and Terry just used their regular names.

Our clique really had it going on. I used to step back occasionally, watch the guys while we were out, and think, *Wow! We're some badass motherfuckers.* But then I would remember that Zach and I were still working at Wendy's. *Man, this shit ain't fuckin' cool at all.*

It did not take long for my grateful attitude toward Wendy's to disintegrate into complete bitter regret. Now when I took people's orders, instead of ringing them up at the register, I pocketed the cash. Every day I also walked out of that place with a big bag of hamburger and chicken patties to stock my refrigerator. I had a dog named Rocky who was growing up not on Purina Dog Chow but on my special blend of Wendy's Chow. He was the best-fed canine in Houston, thanks to jolly old Dave Thomas.

When Z-Boy and I sat around with the other boys in the crew, we complained about our jobs all the time. By the autumn of 1986, at twenty-one years old, I had been working at Wendy's for a couple of years. We didn't last much longer. Z-Boy finally got fed up and quit. Soon after, I was fired for not showing up at all one day.

We were both relieved, but we were so jaded that a very interesting idea developed.

When we were all hanging out smoking some of Toffa's weed, having a typical bull session and making each other laugh, out of nowhere Zach threw out a question: "Why don't we just get some guns and fuckin' rob Wendy's?"

The words hung in the dead silence.

I shook my head, took a hit from the joint, and forgot all about it.

However, what had started off as a harmless joke kept coming up all the time. As our discussions took on a more serious tone, I could tell everyone was thinking the same thing: *Let's explore this concept.* The next thing I knew, we were circling Z-Boy's kitchen table devising an actual plan to knock over Wendy's.

Since Z-Boy and I had worked at the place, we still had a few sets of uniforms each—enough for all of us. The basic idea was that we would dress up as Wendy's employees. Just as the restaurant was being closed up for the night, we would calmly walk in and catch the staff by surprise. We figured the workers would see us and go about their business mopping the floor, counting out the registers, and finishing their closing routine. Then we would rush the counter and jack those suckers for everything they had.

Terry declined to participate. He was a little soft when it came to the criminal aspect of the crew. The rest of us agreed the method was so simple it was genius, but there was only one sure way to find out.

After spending a few more days hashing out the remaining details of our plan, we decided everything was lined up perfectly. We summoned our courage, put our uniforms on, and stepped out into the night. We decided to use Fran's mother's (my aunt

Vallia's) car as our getaway vehicle, and I would be the driver. The Wendy's Bandits were about to strike for the first time.

While I waited in the car with Fran, Z-Boy and Wendell ran in. Less than five minutes later, they raced out and hopped in. I slowly pulled out and drove away nice and easy so as not to draw any attention.

As we headed down the road, Zach said, "Holy shit, Book, that was so easy and smooth. You should've seen it." He was huffing and puffing, so out of breath he could barely tell me about it.

He said they'd casually walked in, and while Wendell had positioned himself near the bathroom hall to stand watch, Z-Boy himself had strolled to the register and started waving around an unloaded .45, demanding they give the money over or he would blow their brains out. Of course, no Wendy's employee would risk life and limb over a little cash. As fast as they could, those suckers behind the counter had stuffed everything from the register into a couple of drive-through sacks and handed them over. Before they even had time to process what had happened, the boys were out and into the car for our getaway.

As I drove away, my heart was pounding. I expected to look in the rearview mirror and see a cop on our tail, sirens blaring, lights flashing.

It wasn't until we got back to my apartment that the extreme paranoia lifted. Now nothing but the excitement of our heist remained. We dumped the cash out of the bags into a messy heap on the table and sorted through it. When we had counted everything up, it was about eight hundred dollars.

We split the money four ways. Our two hundred dollars each wasn't exactly the haul of the century, but when we combined that with the euphoria from what we had just done, we could only come to one conclusion—we *had* to do it again.

Almost immediately, we began revising the plan. That first time had been pretty clean, but it had been a learning experience. The most obvious change was to target something farther away. Hitting our own Wendy's had been a completely risky decision that could have really cost us, but the bitterness Z-Boy and I felt toward that place had blinded our better judgment.

We also decided to pool our money and rent a neutral apartment to serve as a base of operations. At our new hideout located at a complex called Park Village, we could safely stash our loot with no worries of a trail leading to our personal homes.

A few weeks later, we hit for the second time without a hitch. After that, we went on a spree, robbing about twelve Wendy's locations over the next four months. The uniforms always caught the legitimate employees off guard. They simply didn't see it coming until it was way too late.

With each successive robbery, our machine ran better. We never saw ourselves as hard-core criminals but as dudes who merely wanted some cash and weren't interested in menial labor

BOOKER T. HUFFMAN

to get it. We made it a point never to hurt anybody. Aside from the trauma of having the daylights scared out of them by gun-wielding dudes screaming in their faces to hand over money, those people always went home unscathed.

We were lucky none of the Wendy's workers had guns under the counter to retaliate with. For all we knew, they did but froze in the heat of the moment or didn't want to chance being heroes and winding up shot. Our guns were unloaded, but they had no way of knowing that.

It was not long at all before all the major media outlets picked up the story of our bold string of robberies. One morning I walked into a convenience store for a coffee, and after cream-ing, sweetening, and sipping, I almost spit out my java all over the floor. On the front pages of all the local newspapers on the racks were headlines referring to us as the Wendy's Bandits. Seeing the story in print like that was insane. I bought a few copies for the boys, who got a big kick out of it too. We felt like the James Gang from the eighteen hundreds. From then on, we could not wait to pick up the latest edition after each of our hits. We loved to see headlines like "Wendy's Bandits Strike Again!"

The Houston Police Department poured on the pressure by issuing statements on television, offering a five-thousand-dollar reward for any information leading to our capture. Man, that was more cash than we were making. Each haul brought us be-tween a couple hundred and four thousand bucks.

Not one of us was saving a dime either. We threw our cash around as quickly as it came and were not discreet with our new-found wealth. The parties were nonstop. Our generosity even spilled over to Terry. Even though he hadn't done anything to help, sometimes we cut him in on the take just because he was one of us.

We also felt we needed some real flash, and jewelry became the obsession of our spending sprees. I bought big gold and silver ropes and chain necklaces. At one point, I had so much shine around my neck that Mr. T would have stopped dead in his tracks in awe.

While all this was going on, I was still unemployed and sitting around all day while the bills piled up. It seemed like a good idea to connect with Billie and Toffa yet again to see what was up. Sure, robbing Wendy's was bringing in some money, but the way I was spending, it sure was not enough to keep me alive long. I needed another source of income, and selling weed was an easy in. I called my sister and soon suited up to get back in the game.

It felt good to be involved with Billie and Toffa again, but man, I was really burning the candle at both ends. Here I was robbing Wendy's restaurants all over Houston as well as dealing drugs. I had a steady stream of anxiety and was looking over my shoulder at all times, but I was drawn to that lifestyle. After all these years, chasing the adrenaline dragon was an organic part of my life. Financially, the combination of the heists and the dealing was paying off just as planned. I was doing well for myself. But occasionally, I could feel the strings attached to all this fast living. My hectic lifestyle took its toll on me in various ways. Most notably, my attitude was rapidly degenerating. With each passing week, each successive robbery, and each sold bag of weed, the pressure wore my patience thinner.

The boys and I hung out every Sunday at MacGregor Park, one of our official homes away from home. It was always jammed on the weekends with hot chicks and dudes cruising in their cool cars with the tops down and music blasting. If you wanted to see and be seen, this was the place to be. MacGregor Park also attracted gangs and other cliques like ours, and sometimes the whole environment was like a powder keg with a fuse just waiting to be lit.

One Sunday the five of us were at our usual corner in the park, relaxing, feeling on top of the world as the incognito Wendy's Bandits with pockets full of cash as well as pounds of gold and silver around our necks. By that time, Z-Boy and I were almost always strapped with guns just in case anything happened and we needed to be ready.

While we were sitting there taking in the sights and sounds of the park, this one dude came slowly cruising up in a long parade of nice cars. He had a beautiful girl sitting next to him and a really nice gold chain. He smiled and waved to people as if he were grand marshal of the parade.

All of a sudden out of nowhere, this young punk ran up, snatched his gold right off his neck, and screamed, "What are you gonna do about that, you punk motherfucker? Get the fuck out of the car and show me what you're gonna do."

The guy in the car was scared out of his mind and sat there helplessly stunned.

His assailant was practically foaming at the mouth. His little wolf pack of friends looked on, waiting to see if anyone around might get involved.

I was perched on the back of a bench, watching all this unfold, wondering if this fool thought he would try that shit with me. My hands were firmly planted in my pockets and squeezing the twin .38s I was carrying. My gaze was glued to his back. Feeling as agitated as I had been and wanting to release some aggression, I wished he would approach me.

Z-Boy whispered, "Book, it's cool, man."

I took a breath and took my hands out of my pockets.

Nobody had a clue how much I wanted to squeeze those triggers. I had been violated so many different ways throughout the last twenty years that it was as if all my pent-up aggression had channeled into that moment. That guy had become an un-witting symbol of every person who had ever taken advantage of me or abandoned me and of every hardship I had endured.

"Are you okay?" Z-Boy said.

I wasn't sure. I had never experienced anything like this before.

When I went back to my apartment, I almost vomited. When I looked at the mirror, I did not like what I saw. What was I becoming?

Later that night, I tried to sleep but stared at the ceiling until sunrise. I never returned to MacGregor Park, even avoiding driving by at all costs.

After a few weeks, I was cool again and tried to put the whole gun incident behind me. Soon enough, it was business as usual. I cut the boys in on my deal with Toffa. We were selling a shitload of weed and raking in the money. Still, it was never enough. Once again, it was time for a trip to Wendy's for a Frosty and cash.

It had been about a month since our last robbery, and I decided it was time for me to get my feet wet and actually go into Wendy's with Zach for the first time. Since our first job, I had always stayed on the fringe of all the madness by driving, which was probably a passive way of saying, "I'm too scared to go in and do that shit with you guys. I'll be the designated getaway driver instead." I'm sure the other guys saw it that way too but didn't care. Everyone knew how important a dependable driver was, making sure those wheels were ready to go. When I told them what I wanted to do, they each gave me a quick fist bump and a hug.

Z-Boy was extra pumped for the night. Since day one, he had been telling me I should see what it was all about. "Hell fuckin' yeah, Book. I knew it was only a matter of time before you'd get hungry for a taste of the action. It's gonna get crazy in there, but you're more than ready."

He was right. I was curious what it would be like going inside, and by this time I was completely committed to the crew. So on a rainy night in 1987, I put on my Wendy's outfit and joined Zach, Fran, and Wendell in a four-strong Wendy's Bandits run-in at a franchise location in Northside.

Since no one was sitting out in the car as the designated driver, we decided to park on the other side of the gate of an apartment complex next to the restaurant. We knew it was a great spot to leave the car because it would make it a lot harder to chase us. Any pursuer would have to climb over or go around that gate.

After several deep breaths, we got out of the car, leapt over the fence, and calmly walked to the side entrance of the building. As we made our approach, two employees took out the garbage. We slipped in right behind them on their way back in.

Each of us had a certain position to get into so that all the entrances and counter area were covered. Once arranged and settled, we proceeded to pull out our guns and get down to business.

Zach took over and started screaming, "Get the fuck down, or I'll kill somebody. You motherfuckers, get the fuck down."

I wasn't at all prepared for the chaos of the scene. A few trembling customers still sat in the restaurant. One of them had fries hanging out of his wide-open mouth.

For the first time, it hit me that I had stepped out of who I was and become something much different. My entire life, I had been the one getting bullied and pushed around, and here I was doing it to these people.

While I stood there, chaos was going down all around me. I snapped out of it just in time to see Fran jump over the counter and swipe all the cash from the registers as the rest of us nervously looked in every direction, waving our guns like madmen. It was almost too much to handle. It seemed we were in there forever, though it was only about three minutes in total.

In some of the early robberies, the guys who had gone in had worn stockings over their heads, but they had since stopped and we all went totally visible. There were no security cameras, and no one in the restaurant knew us. Still, I kept my head down as much as possible. If there was one thing I always realized, it was that I had a distinct, memorable face. The last thing I wanted was to be recognized someday while out and about.

Another less-than-brainy move was the fact that we had girls around. I was seeing this black-Asian girl everyone called Red because of her bronze complexion. Red's best friend, Robin, was Z-Boy's girl. Aside from the boys in the crew, our girls were the only two people on the planet who knew what we had been up to as the Wendy's Bandits. They watched in the wings as we planned and carried out our robberies and sold marijuana, and they became increasingly excited as the media frenzy surrounding the Bandits grew.

During shows like *Texas Outlaws*, Crime Stoppers ads constantly ran, reminding people to identify us for that five-thousand-dollar reward. One time when it came up, I could have sworn I saw a spark in Robin's eyes.

The pressure was building. After this most recent escapade, we made our way back to the hideout at Park Village and divvied up the take, which was a thousand dollars total. To unwind after all the commotion, excitement, and stress, we took our shares and partied all night. We went to a bar to wash down double-tall glasses of Hennessy, Cognac, and Jack and Cokes until closing time, then headed to the apartment to smoke weed until dawn.

For weeks after that robbery, we took a break from the action. One evening Red and I made plans for a special little lunch date the next day. I would join Zach afterward to take care of some usual weed business—both selling and smoking. Then I would take it back home to crash for the night.

The events of April 9, 1987 came out of nowhere like a shot to the head, and they sent me straight from the streets to prison. When the long arm of the law took hold of me and smashed me down to the ground, I knew exactly what the score was.

Now here I was in prison, fulfilling Mom's prophecy: *If you don't stop, you'll end up dead or in jail.*

I alone had gotten myself into this, and it was time to make up my mind how I would handle it. I could let the system eat me alive, become a bitter institutionalized young black man, and blame my problems on everyone else. Or I could accept my time for what it was—my responsibility.

I was determined to pick myself up and rise above it all one way or another. I would do something special with my life—something my mother would have been proud of. I carried that philosophy with me, like Booker T's Commandments, at all times. It was way beyond time to develop a productive approach to my stay on the inside. When I woke up my first morning in Pack 2, I would do so with a fresh perspective and a promise: I would use my life to make big things happen.

ENTERING THE SYSTEM

At six in the morning, my first wake-up call at Pack 2 came like an unwelcome slap to the face. As the lights kicked on and the guards loudly made their presence known, I just lay there in my rack staring at the ceiling, trying to clear my mind. My eyes stung with each blink, and when I heard the grumblings and yawns of the inmates, I knew I really was in prison. It wasn't just a nightmare after all. Groggy from having slept no more than an hour or two, I got up to make my rack like everybody else.

The first order of business before finding out exactly what kind of work I would be doing at Pack 2 was to make my way to the chow hall for breakfast. Let there be no mistaking it: prison food is terrible. It is nothing but the cheapest run-of-the-mill, mass-produced slop the government can allow to be served up piping hot on a tray. My unceremonious inaugural meal was a serving-spoon-sized splatter of creamy chipped beef on two pieces of white toast, otherwise known as shit on a shingle. It looked like vomit and tasted even worse.

After choking down my breakfast, I wondered what was in store for me. The answer came quicker than I expected.

"All right, come on and get moving. Time to hit the field."

The guards barked orders, and the other inmates grudgingly formed two single-file lines.

The field? I thought. *What the fuck is that?*

We were shackled together and loaded into the back of a big, covered work truck. A few miles from the prison, we stopped. Chain gang–style, we walked off the truck and practically fell into each other, igniting a falling line of domino inmates. As we steadied ourselves, I felt the hot sun focusing in overhead and broke into a sweat. Slowly, clumsily, we staggered into a giant field, where they unchained us. The scene was pretty close to ones from the movie *Cool Hand Luke*.

Oh, this is the field, I thought.

The guards, seated high on white horses with their rifles at the ready, directed us to a pile of axes, hatchets, and saws. "Get to it, boys. You know what to do."

Even though I did not have a clue what to do, I learned pretty quickly. A few yards in the distance were trees, stumps, wood chips, and sawdust everywhere. It was time for some good old-fashioned, backbreaking labor. Great.

For hours, I chopped, hacked, and pulled stuff apart and hauled it away until blisters the size of quarters had formed on every inch of my gloveless hands. The only break came at noon, when we were loaded into the truck, taken all the way back to

Pack 2, and served these awful soybean patties along with some greens and corn, which were all grown on the premises by the inmates. The second we finished that miserable crap, we headed straight back to the grind of the field for four more hours.

Needless to say, after getting my first taste of the brutal work detail, I was not thrilled at the long-term prospect of this new routine. The whole time I was out there swinging my axe, I was obsessed with finding a solution to this dismal new dilemma known as labor.

All right, Booker, you're in a shit situation, I thought. *You can get out of it. How are you going to do it?* That became a mantra in my head from the time I woke up each day until I lay down sixteen hours later.

One saving grace during my time on the chain gang was encountering Butler, a black guy from Dallas who was in for a drug beef. He was willing to laugh at his situation and take everything in stride, which reminded me of myself. After just a few days of being out in the field together, we became friends.

One particular day, Butler invited me to one of the countertops in the dorm and offered to share one of his spreads of chili, cheese, and crackers. "Book," he said, "we're definitely brothers from another mother."

I wondered how a smart and charismatic dude like Butler had landed in prison, but I was sure glad he had. Without his carefree attitude making me laugh every step and chop of the way out there in the sun and under the watchful eyes of those guards, I might have cracked.

I especially loved watching Butler play ball. Pack 2 had recreation time after dinner in a decent little gym, where we shot around and played pickup basketball games to let off some steam. Those courts were where Butler really came alive, and I was amazed by the display he would put on.

Butler schooled everyone, and the trash talk he spewed the whole time made me die laughing. "Come on, boy, what you gonna do, huh? I'm about to pass your ass with a 360 spin to your right, and you still won't stop it. I'm the motherfuckin' soul train."

Then he would do exactly what he'd said, dumbfounding everyone.

Butler was something else. Everyone in the prison knew when it came to ballin' he was the dude you wanted on your team. If you didn't have him, you were going to lose.

I was happy I'd made a solid friend, but I was still constantly plotting to remove myself from the daily grind in the field. Butler helped me out by explaining some of the various ins and outs of Pack 2. Most notably, I learned that one of the privileges inside those walls was to get a job. It could have been anything from cultivating the prison vegetable garden, to doing general custodial duties, to working on the kitchen team. A job not only could get me out of working in the field but also would come with many perks. An inmate with a job of value could barter his services with other prisoners for commissary items, cigarettes, and even social status. It also helped curry favor with the guards, who generally respected and got along better with the guys who worked hard at their jobs. In some cases, it helped guys move up the ladder to even better, more important positions.

Sometimes, though, it was not even necessary to earn your job through hard work. If the guards and the inmates simply liked you, you could get one. It was all about being cool, fitting in, and knowing how to work the social element of the system. If you didn't conduct yourself the right way around people from the start, rest assured you would be trying to dig yourself out of a hole halfway down to China for the remainder of your bid.

Of course, I decided to work the social angle. The guards had noticed the difference in me compared to some of the other dudes. They saw my even-tempered disposition and the manners my mother had instilled in me. My steady stream of "yes, sir," "no, sir," "please," and "thank you" was more than enough to bring the right attention my way, just as I had planned. For the first time in my life, I felt as if I was in the accelerated program in school and all the teachers supported me.

Even though I was in prison, I focused on the positives one by one to keep my mind together until an eventual parole date came my way. When I soon landed a job, I knew I was definitely on the right path. I was happy as hell to get into the laundry room and work with linens and wool as opposed to laboring in that unbearable field, swinging those blister-producing axes.

A little part of me felt bad for leaving Butler alone out there, but he was happy to see me move up in the ranks. "Hey, brother," he said, "just don't forget about us little folks when you become a bigwig in the house."

Working the laundry was a cool job, and I really appreciated the opportunity to explore every aspect of it. Even as a little kid, I had loved starching up my jeans and getting that deep crease down the front of the pant legs with the iron. Now as a big boy I was running the laundry, learning the pressing machines and various new cleaning techniques with chemicals and detergents. As a result, I had the whitest, crispest, freshest clothes and sheets. I gave Butler's the same treatment. Our gear was straight.

When the other guys caught wind, the bartering came into play. Now that they had their boy Booker T in the laundry, I was in business and everything was negotiable. If some of the other dudes were bumming around and needed new clothes or just wanted theirs to be as sharp as mine and ahead of schedule, we did a quick trade. They might give me some pastries or spread ingredients like Ramen noodles, cheese, or cans of tuna.

Butler would always see the deals going down and marvel at my scam. "Shit, man, you're the godfather of laundry town. Can I be your general?"

He knew he already was. I would keep some of the stuff for Butler and myself or trade it for cigarettes, a habit I'd picked up again, or sell it for pocket cash. It was a great setup and no different from the way life worked on the outside. If there was one thing I could count on, both in prison and in the free world, it was that one hand always washed the other.

Now that I had my laundry role, it was easier to relax and check out the lay of the land inside Pack 2. When going into a prison environment, the best approach is to keep your back against the wall so you know it's covered. As time moves on, you can slowly decide the best way to venture out into the population. It didn't take me long to understand the social dynamics with certain inner circles and learn who was cool and which players to avoid.

My mother had always said something that proved true in prison: "You've got to know when to speak up and when to shut up." You definitely did not want to go running into a place like Pack 2 and step on toes and draw attention. In the event that a situation did come your way, you had to handle it swiftly and strongly.

After I had been in Pack 2 for a couple of months, I got to see what it was like when a new guy came in and didn't understand how to handle things or stand up for himself. Sometimes those dudes would pay off an established inmate with commissary items, cash, or cigarettes in exchange for protection. This was called riding with someone.

When I first entered prison, I had no idea what that meant. I sure as hell would not have gone for it anyway. The moment I walked into Pack 2, as green as they come, I understood this was a dog-eat-dog scenario and prepared to do anything necessary to survive. Armed with my street knowledge and fearless attitude toward anyone stupid enough to cross me, I skated through Pack 2 without major incident.

But on occasion, I did see others have a hard time. When this new white kid named Jason came in, he was obviously far out of his element. He didn't have the slightest clue where he was or what to do.

One day, apparently Jason figured out how to find protection. "Hey, Booker," he said, "I don't feel so safe around here, you know? I was wondering if I could ride with you."

Man, I hadn't seen that one coming. In my lifetime, no one had ever asked me for protection. It was kind of embarrassing.

I found out this black guy named Vernon had smelled the kid's trepidation like blood in a shark tank and was messing with him. Jason was scared out of his mind that something might happen to him. I could see the deathly concern in his eyes when he asked me for help.

Feeling bad for the boy, I reluctantly agreed. "Don't worry. Just get yourself to the commissary and get me some bear claws as fast as your little legs can move. I've got you."

This cat Vernon was a hardened prisoner currently in Pack 2 for his third bid, obviously not having gotten the point the first two times. I saw him around but did not talk to him, was not his boy, and definitely was not afraid of him. By now, I was twenty-two years old, six foot two, and well over two hundred pounds. I always walked around feeling there wasn't a dude in the dorm I couldn't whip.

It was easy to see the others felt it too. They would all watch as I repped out my usual five hundred push-ups before bed, looking at each other as if they were thinking, *Damn*. During the day it was as if a sign hung from my neck, stating, I Am Booker T, and I Have Zero Patience for Bullshit, so Don't Fuck with Me. This worked out just great for everyone involved, especially me.

Without realizing Jason had a guardian angel, Vernon trash-talked him one night in the dorm within my earshot. "Hey, boy, how come you ain't got a beat-down yet, huh? Who said you can just walk around here like you want? There's a price to pay for motherfuckers like you. If you don't cash in tomorrow and get me some cigarettes, your ass is on the line."

Jason did the right thing and kept his head down, ignoring him.

Vernon didn't like that at all. "Don't you hear me, boy? I'm talking to you."

I had heard enough. It was time to let everyone, specifically Vernon, in on my arrangement with Jason. Letting out a sigh, I rolled from my rack, sat up, put on my boots, and took off my shirt. Staring directly at Vernon, I stood and made a little announcement. "All right, everybody, listen up. This is how it goes."

That silenced all the inmates. Even Butler was taken aback by what was unfolding, because he wasn't really aware of my agreement with Jason. I knew he would have my back in a heartbeat, but in a situation like this he knew to sit back and let his boy take care of his own business until otherwise necessary.

"This three-time piece-of-shit loser sitting here is about to be a prime example of what happens to anyone stupid enough to fuck around with Jason. It ain't happening no more, understand?"

Everybody looked on to see what would happen.

By that time, Vernon's jaw had dropped, and he ran to his rack.

Thinking we'd been on the verge of throwing down, I stood there among the boys and called to Vernon. "Come out, man. This is what you wanted, right? You wanted to kick somebody's ass. Well, come and kick mine, bro."

There was no response.

Seeing how well my point had been made, I decided to let Vernon off the hook. He was ruined from that point on anyway, looking like a complete fool in front of the house.

I could not have been happier. Even Butler walked up and nudged me while I was making a victory spread of Ramen noodles, chicken, and cheese with crushed-up crackers, which we shared over our usual laugh.

"That was right on, Book. I thought I was going to shit my pants when you went off. I think old Vernon actually did."

In one moment, without having lifted a finger, I had shown the entire dorm exactly what I was made of. And I'll let you in on a little secret—I was bluffing. The truth of the whole matter was that because of the trouble I would get into, I didn't want to fight. I didn't want to lose my job and get extra time. No way. Although I was ready to swing for the fences, my intention was to overwhelm Vernon with a ferocious bark and back his ass down without the conflict coming to blows. When it worked, I thought, *Whew, that was a close one.*

Just for added measure for the show, while Vernon brooded on his rack in a crumpled mess, I decided to sit on my bed and stare across the room at him for an hour or two. I would say he got the message. From that point on, my status within Pack 2 was established. Neither Jason nor I had another problem with anybody during the remainder of our bids.

After about four months in Pack 2, the one-year anniversary of my arrest came up. Despite how agonizingly slow it had seemed while I lived it day by day, I could not believe so much time had passed since that fateful evening of April 9, 1987. That's the thing about prison. All you truly pay attention to is time. You're fully aware of the days and the pain of being inside, severed from the world.

My grip on the outside had pretty much faded away by that point, and I was becoming institutionalized. Sure, the letters from Billie Jean and Red still came, but they were fewer and further between. I understood, though, and simply accepted it for what it was. I did not feel like communicating with anybody anyway.

Being in prison was a realistic example of *out of sight, out of mind*. Life didn't stop out there just because mine was on hold. I was the one who had slipped through due to the idiocy of choosing to be a Wendy's Bandit.

The only option I could see now was to keep my chin up and my nose to the grindstone. Otherwise, bitterness would devour my spirit. With this awareness making more sense by the day, I continued to focus on being constructive while waiting out my sentence.

I had been doing great with the laundry and enjoyed all the benefits that came along with the job, but it was growing a little stale. I wondered if there were more productive or worthwhile things to apply myself to. I wasn't sure what I would land my sights on, but I looked around at all the possibilities.

After the episode with Vernon, nothing was beyond my reach. The guards' and inmates' ever-growing respect made me feel like the captain of a high school football team or something. Everyone knew my name, wanted to talk, and even offered to help get me into other programs or jobs.

During some of my conversations, the guys mentioned a weight lifting team, so I asked for details. My mind raced considering such a perfectly suited avenue.

I had first noticed the weight room while watching Butler destroy everyone on the basketball court in the gym during recreation time. It had a full arsenal of barbells and dumbbells with benches, squat racks, and all the cable pulley machines. I had been working out ever since, capturing a lot of the essence of those old intense sessions with Lash. Over the months I was in Pack 2, I had steadily put on about 30 pounds. I was up to around 225 pounds of pure, lean mass when I found out about the competitive lifting team.

The other guys in the gym took notice of how strong I was. "Damn, Booker, why don't you come on board the team? We could use you, man, and it counts as a job."

That's all I needed to hear.

But there were two problems. The first obvious issue was the fact that I still worked in the laundry room. It wasn't as if I could simply transfer to another position at my own will. Always being the pragmatic thinker, I found a solution.

Pack 2 had a General Education Development (GED) program for inmates to pursue a high school equivalency certification. If they accepted me in the program, they would release me from my duties in the laundry room for the necessary class time. This meant I could not only redeem myself for dropping out of school but also free my schedule to join the weight lifting team.

When I applied to the GED program, they welcomed me in with open arms. As great as it felt to be accepted there, I had to address a second issue to join the weight lifting team. All team members had to have a minimum ten-year prison bid to qualify for competition. I clocked in at only two concurrently running five-year terms.

I got a little creative and came up with a less-than-honest solution. *Well,* I thought, *since two sets of five equals ten, I'm good, right?* So I lied to the guard in charge, telling him I met the ten-year eligibility. Due to my stand-up status, they put me on the squad without any further investigation.

Classes started almost immediately for me. Entering the GED program was probably the best decision I made while at Pack 2. There was an actual classroom complete with rows of desks, a blackboard, a globe, and a wall-mounted pencil sharpener. The only thing missing was Ms. Hughes's ass. I sat through all the standard science, math, and social studies courses and even had homework assignments due each day.

After class was over, I went straight to the gym, where I got to complement my studying efforts with good old heavy metal. It felt great to be exercising my mind and my body, all the while repaying my debt to society. I knew this was all preparation for a better life when my release would come. This was exactly the type of productive pursuit I had been looking for all along. I would go back into society with a whole different perspective and appearance, and I would have so much more to offer the outside world than when I had been taken away.

But in order to make sure that was the case, I had to stay on my toes. For the first time since my mother had been alive, people were telling me exactly what had to be done and when or there would be repercussions. Because I had been released of laundry room duties to go to school, I had to meet the grade eligibility requirement to stay on the team. It was the life of a student-athlete. If my grades went below a solid C and the teacher knew I was not focusing, I would lose everything and be sent back down to the dirty socks, the piles of sheets, and the pressing machine. That was not going to happen. I was certain to get my work done and hit those beckoning weights as if there were no tomorrow. It was all that mattered.

I did what was required of me in the classroom, but when it came to the team I was an overachiever. On the bench for the first time since the days with my brother and Darryl, I tossed up

265 pounds. On the squat, I managed 335.

Although those figures are respectable for anyone, on a competitive level I needed to make some serious progress. Within months of throwing that iron around as hard as I could, I watched my bench climb to 315 and my squat to 405.

I was in a good mental place when something inconceivable happened. Just when I thought all the correspondence from the world beyond had ended, an envelope from Billie Jean arrived. The message chilled me to the bone.

Billie had forwarded me a letter from the Texas Department of Family and Protective Services (DFPS) in Houston. They were attempting to locate me so I could take custody of Brandon before he was entered into their adoption system and possibly lost to me forever. Apparently, Angela had given him up to DFPS for reasons unknown, although I had my suspicions she was overwhelmed being a single mother at such a young age. Since I had been roaming for such a long time with no steady residence, the department had lost considerable time tracking down my last known location to Billie's, where they had sent the letter.

I could not believe it. A wave of confusion, rage toward Angela, and fear rushed over me. My emotions were all over the place, but I soon calmed down and realized what a hypocrite I was being. Who was I to complain and point fingers? I was sitting in prison for armed robbery. I had run out on both Angela and Brandon years earlier. I was disgusted with myself.

The letter was useless aside from giving me a haunting awareness that somewhere a frightened, innocent boy was abandoned and alone. He had to have felt the same way I had after my mother's death—and I was responsible.

I called Billie to talk about Brandon's situation, but she couldn't do anything because she was not a legal guardian.

Like a parasite, the news ate me alive. I knew the minute my release came, I would not rest until I found Brandon. Until then, I had to accept the situation, press on, and stay strong.

My resolve was quickly tested. Although it was something Butler and I had discussed over the year or so we'd known each other, I had forgotten his time was coming to be paroled. When we were in the dorm playing a game of chess, two guards walked in and told him to pack up.

He smiled. "Shit, Book, I'm outta here! Help me pack up, man."

We went to his rack, and I watched my only true friend rifle through his belongings for what to keep and what to give away. In prison, we started with nothing and left with the same. He had canned meats, crackers, cookies, and a few magazines, which he handed over to me. Then he stood and looked at me. "Take care of yourself. You're gonna do great things someday. And you'll always be my brother from another mother."

We gave each other a brief handshake hug, and just like that, Butler disappeared through the doors with a final peace sign out. I would never see him again.

I felt bittersweet over my friend's freedom. His long-awaited gain was my loss, but that was just the way it went on the inside. I imagined him on the outside, smiling in his newfound independence. It made me laugh out loud and think of my own not-too-distant future. I knew my day was coming soon, and that would keep me going.

FREE AT LAST

After being in Pack 2 for just over nine months, I knew virtually everything about the place and how it ran from the bottom up and the inside out. Prison life there in our Navasota home was not as tense as I had expected. You had all walks of life in there, from blacks to black Muslims to Puerto Ricans to Mexicans to whites, who were a minority in there, to a small sect of openly gay dudes who walked around without incident. For the most part, everybody congregated in their own circles and kept pretty cool about things, but just to make sure, the guards established different TV times for each group.

At night we had the usual activities, such as playing cards and dominoes, drinking coffee, and smoking cigarettes and joints if you had them. Peace was usually maintained, but with so many different races, colors, and creeds under one roof, once in a while we had an eruption. Sometimes we had random, nonfatal beatings and shankings over trivial things like line cutting at the chow hall, cheating in cards, or unpaid debts of commissary items or cigarettes.

When something was about to go down, I would see all the guys lined up on one side or gathered around in big circles. I could feel it in the air. However, not every event came with warning signs.

One night we were all sitting around in the dorm watching television, and even though it was the time set aside for the black group to have our channel on, a few Mexicans in the back were mouthing off. They did not like the movie we were watching, and with the already extremely low levels of tolerance among inmates, the ticking time bomb exploded. Within seconds, chairs were flying and dudes were punching and kicking. Fury swirled like a tornado, gathering momentum by the second, engulfing everything in its path.

I sat as calmly as possible in the middle of it. I believed anyone who got near me would think twice about doing anything rash, and I was right. One dude came running in my direction, recognized who I was, and took the long way around as if a protective force field surrounded me.

Before I knew it, the guards were smashing in with their riot gear and giant Plexiglas shields, throwing tear gas all over the place. Within two minutes, the dorm was locked down and all the inmates were incapacitated.

Afterward, the guards brought us in one by one for questioning. They wanted to know how it had all started, who we had seen do what, and what our own personal involvement had been. When it was my turn, the code of the street kicked in. I was not saying a word.

"Man, I didn't see shit and don't know anything. You guys know how I am in here. Nobody bothered me, and I kept cool. All I remember was some commotion started over the TV."

That's all I had to say. Without mentioning names or groups, I saved face not only with the guys in the dorm but with the guards as well. My answer was respectful toward them and gave them something to go on, which was good enough for them and everyone else. Once again, I was out of a jam and right back up on a pedestal. And that's exactly where I liked to be, especially with my parole board hearing coming up.

I kept quiet about the hearing among the other prisoners, especially the weight lifters, since I'd gotten on the team under false pretenses about the duration of my sentence. When the time came, I was led into this tiny room where a panel of four supervisors sat at a table facing one lone chair. They smiled, motioned for me to come in, said hello, and told me to take a seat.

I sat and smiled back, trying not to stare at them too much while collecting my racing thoughts. I pressed my sweaty palms firmly against my knees to keep them dry. This was it. The next phase of my life would be decided there and then. Adrenaline pumped through every inch of my body as the interview began.

"Mr. Huffman, do you feel remorseful for the crime you committed against society?"

I did not need to think about it for a second. I launched into an automatic answer that had been building inside me since that first night in Harris County. As if my mother herself sat by my side and guided my thoughts, I told the parole board every detail of the hows and whys of the Wendy's Bandits. I explained that I had received no guidance after Mom had passed, had hung with the wrong crowd, and had gotten involved with drugs. From April 9, 1987, until that very moment in front of them, I had been thinking about what had brought me here. I continued to speak in detail about all the sleepless nights I had spent staring at the ceilings of various institutions seeking an opportunity to redeem myself. When they asked why I'd taken the plea bargain instead of contesting the charges, I said my guilt made it impossible to weasel out; I had to make restitution for my actions.

The board was engrossed and asked several basic follow-up questions: "Would you ever offend and break the law again? How would you change your life for the better to benefit society?"

I had ready answers. I told them all about Brandon, how things went really badly with him, and my intentions upon being released. "I'm going to pick myself up from the ground when I leave this facility and get a job. Then I'm going to find my son and do what's right. He's out there somewhere all alone, and it's my responsibility to give him the father he needs and deserves."

One member of the panel, a woman, was visibly moved. When it was all over, as bizarre as it might sound, I felt cleansed. Sitting there in front of those people and telling my entire story without any bullshit was like a confession in church or something. For better or for worse, letting all that out from beginning to end helped ease some of the hurt, guilt, and pressure that had been locked inside me since my mother had died.

As I stood, the panel thanked me. The guards led me back to the dorm.

I sat on my rack, my head hanging. I felt totally drained, hoping I'd said the right things in there. Some of the other guys filed into the cell after recreation time was over. They could tell by how quiet I was that I did not really feel like talking. The next few weeks in the dorm were the longest stretch of time I did in prison.

Thankfully I had something to keep my mind busy. I had yet to reach the winners' platform for the weight lifting team. I had been at it hard for about eight months, and in another two I would compete in my first exhibition. By now, my bench press had soared to 385 pounds, and just four weeks out from the competition, I made an attempt at 405 pounds.

I was so excited to get under that weight and test myself for the first time. The plates on each side made the bar slightly bend in the middle. After psyching myself up and taking several deep breaths, I lay back on the bench and nodded at my spotter for a liftoff on the count of three. I held it up for a split second, then slowly lowered the crushing poundage to my chest. In one swift burst, I pressed it straight up. I did it—405 pounds!

All the guys cheered, and I stood and gave everybody high fives and hugs. I was proud of myself for working so hard for so long toward a constructive goal. It was the single greatest achievement in my life to date. I put my hands on my hips, trying to catch my breath. An uncontrollable smile stretched across my face as I stared at that intimidating bar sitting on the rack with those giant plates still noticeably bouncing.

Just then the doors to the gym swung open, and two of the guards came walking my way. The hairs on the back of my neck stood straight up.

One of them announced, "Huffman, get your stuff. You're a free man."

Well, I'll be! I had served a total of only nineteen months of two concurrently running five-year sentences. For whatever reason—maybe my upstanding behavior and some good old-fashioned luck—the parole board had decided it was my time.

I almost collapsed as euphoria coursed through me. I had dreamed of this moment for nineteen months. I did not know how to react or what to say. "Get the fuck out of here! Seriously? Come on, man. Seriously?"

The guard nodded and flashed a tiny smile. This was the real deal. I was going home.

Having just accomplished the colossal lifting feat in front of my team, I got some mixed reactions that resulted in an awkward, anticlimactic moment.

"Hey, man," one of the guys said, "how in the hell did you manage to come up on parole so soon? That could only be possible if you had a bid like half as long as your ten years."

I had to tell these boys who'd become my friends about my lie to get onto the team. They shook their heads and laughed it off. Yes, I was letting them down, but they were proud to see one of their own return to the outside.

All that was left to do in the dorm before checking out was to pack up what little belongings I had in my locker and say my good-byes, just as Butler had done not long before.

As I sat there pulling out my stash of commissary foods and spices, cigarettes, magazines, and stuff like that, I thought, *Why don't I just give this shit away? I don't need it.* So that's what I did. I walked around like Santa Claus with my bag and handed out whatever each of my buddies wanted as we shook hands and said good-bye.

Just before I walked out the door, I stopped and turned for a last wave. Everyone clapped for me. Just a touch sad, I smiled.

From the dorm, I was led down the same hall I had walked after first arriving at Pack 2. I was sent into a small holding cell with four other dudes who were going home too. We could not contain our smiles as we changed into our street clothes, which we hadn't seen since the days we were arrested. Mine were ridiculously tight due to the weight I had gained. Then we waited for the next step.

Within a few minutes, the guards came to put us on a bus, unshackled, for the trip to Houston—but not before we walked past a rifle-toting guard on his white horse.

"I'll see you when you get back, Huffman."

I smiled and waved, glancing at that motherfucker's face for the last time. He was just taking a parting dig, but the last laugh would be all mine when I proved him wrong and stayed on the outside for good.

We all boarded the bus, and it finally hit me—I was a free man. As we pulled away from the curb, I watched Pack 2 slowly disappear behind us. I thought of the self-discipline prison had given me along with the confidence of being a natural leader people could trust. My remorse for my crime and for losing Brandon had slowly changed me. Day in and day out, the broken clay fragments of a confused boy had been shaped into a strong, twenty-three-year-old man.

Although the system had pulled me in and proceeded to drain what little spirit I had, now I realized they had refilled me with passion. In many ways, I felt like King Arthur after he lost his purpose in life and sent the Knights of the Round Table in search of the Holy Grail to save him. After a long and treacherous journey, Sir Percival returned with the grail. As Arthur sipped from the cup, he said, "I didn't know how empty was my soul, until it was filled." Amen, brother. I was King Booker.

The bus pulled in for a rest stop at some gas station in the middle of nowhere. It's funny how you take for granted little things like simply walking up and down the aisle of a convenience store. Looking at all the chips and candy bars took me back to childhood when buying a Snickers and a Coke had made my entire day. On the way out of Pack 2, each of us had been given some cash. It felt good to be out and about with a few bucks in my pocket, and I couldn't resist buying my old favorite snack combo before returning to the bus for the last leg of the journey home.

As I rested my head against the bus window and we neared Houston, my anxiety started to build. One of the main concerns of the parole board had been about where I would be staying and the conditions of that place. I had established that Billie Jean's was the place I'd be going. She was the only one who had been there for me throughout my whole prison ordeal. By now Red, tired of waiting for a convict's release, was long gone. Over the course of my many phone conversations with Billie while at Pack 2, she had agreed to take me in.

What made me nervous about Billie, though, was the fact that she was still in the game, running with Toffa, as if time had stood still while I'd been gone. You can imagine the trepidation I felt over the prospect of moving back into that atmosphere, possibly risking my parole. If I fell victim to past demons, I would be thrown into Pack 2 faster than a supervising officer could say, "Violation!" I was determined to prove that guard on the horse wrong. I would never return.

We finally pulled in to the bus station in downtown Houston, and my will was tested much earlier than I had anticipated.

Apparently, all the gamers knew exactly what the prison bus looked like and perched around like wretched vultures seeking fresh kill. As I walked down the bus steps, those dudes addressed me. "Hey, man, you need some coke? A girl? You wanna smoke a joint?"

I waved them off, focused straight ahead, and kept walking. With my bag in hand, I walked to the bus terminal waiting area. There was Billie looking around for me.

"Hey, girl! What you doing around here?"

She gave me a big, tight hug and held on for a while. "Junior! You look great, boy."

We had an awesome little reunion and were so happy to see each other.

"Come on," she said. "Let's get you the hell out of here."

That sounded good to me.

Man, I was back. It was so strange to be riding in a car again in Houston as if the whole ordeal of the last year and a half had never happened. Billie drove me to the house she was now renting in South Park, literally only five minutes away from my old neighborhood.

Now that I was out in the real world, one thought persistently struck me: *Okay, now what am I going to do?* I had been sent to prison for robbing my last place of employment. How could I run right out and look for a job? I was a well-known ex-con with only a GED and some prison laundry experience.

I knew finding gainful employment was crucial to being on parole and eventually taking custody of Brandon, but it was easier said than done. Fortunately, the parole office was satisfied with my many lies about hitting the pavement every morning and knocking on doors seeking work. Sooner or later, though, I had to do something.

Life continued while I sat around and simply watched the daily dirt of my sister's and Toffa's dealings. The temptation was strong, and I felt myself being pulled right back into the spinning maelstrom of the game. For a hot minute there, I was selling weed again to some of the same old tired faces, which both depressed and terrified me. These people were not going anywhere in life, but if I didn't watch out, *I* would be going somewhere all right—back to prison.

Then something divine intervened and woke me right up. One day I got a letter from Child Protective Services telling me Brandon was in foster care and asking whether I was interested in seeing him.

Wow, I thought. *This is fuckin' crazy. I gotta do something about this.*

I did not even know how the letter had found its way to me, because Billie had moved from the address over a year earlier. It was simply meant to be. Angela was nowhere to be found, and I could imagine her ripping and running somewhere without thinking about her son. The letter went on to mention how there was only so much time to respond before Brandon would be lost in the system forever. According to the deadline noted, I still had time.

Before responding, I took a good, hard look in the mirror. I traced the lines of my face and looked down in a moment of self-realization. *What are you going to do, Booker? What kind of man are you? Stop thinking of yourself, and step the fuck up.*

As if she were standing right behind me looking over my shoulder, my mother immediately came to mind. Thinking of how she had raised eight kids all by herself, I had my moment of truth. I knew what she would do. The right thing. And that was the only conclusion that made sense.

There was no more time to hesitate. I made the call.

The lady on the other end of the line invited me to the offices for an interview.

At the meeting, I told the caseworker of my recent past and how my life had completely turned around and that I was interested in supporting Brandon. Although I did not have a job yet, I assured her one was right around the corner and I had quite a few thousand dollars in savings set aside in case of an emergency. The last part was an absolute lie. The caseworker said having proof of a substantial bank account along with the promise of employment was enough to get the ball rolling.

I was already working out a plan to back up my financial claim. Billie and Toffa still maintained an outside apartment for their weed, and no one knew I had this information. The little voice in my head was telling me this could be my one shot. There was no turning back.

So in my best Robin Hood tribute, I slipped into the empty apartment and stole the entire five-pound stash of weed from the rich Jamaicans to give to the poor—me. It was the last time

I ever stole anything. Although Toffa would be pissed, he would recover and go right back to business. No real harm done.

After selling off all that dope to the public through my cousin, I pocketed just over three thousand dollars. Now that I had the savings I had lied about, all that remained was to find a job to sustain it. I decided to call on Lash once again to see what was up.

My big brother was excited to hear from me. "I'll definitely help you get back on your feet," he said. "All I ask is that whatever job we get you—sweeping floors, washing dishes, or digging ditches—you give it your all. You gotta pay your dues and walk a straight line."

How could I say no to that? It was as fair and realistic a deal as anyone could ask for.

He recommended I apply for a job doing security for a company that had an opening at Pier Club Apartments. Lash himself had held the same position just a few months before but had since moved on.

The idea of it was pretty funny. I would be protecting people's property from guys like I once was. On the application, I came to this question: "Have you ever been convicted of a crime?"

I wondered, *Should I tell the truth?* I thought about it for all of two seconds and checked "No." I rationalized it away and convinced myself it was the only way. I figured once they got to know me and really like me, they wouldn't look into my past anyway. I mean, it wasn't as if I was applying for a job at the White House where there would be investigative background checks.

I turned the paper in to the manager and was hired on the spot. So began my role as Pier Club Apartment neighborhood watchman. I was even given a free apartment, which was an unexpected bonus that helped stretch my paycheck.

Six months later, my assumption backfired. My employer certainly did check my background, and just like that I was kicked out the door.

I did manage to jam my foot back in and keep the door open just enough to discover another opportunity. Being the smiling and helpful dude I was, I had gotten to know the guy who ran the apartment complex, Bruce Gasarch. With Lash's personal recommendation, which carried a lot of weight, Bruce hired me as a maintenance man.

That job was great, and I was really happy to learn all kinds of skills, such as carpentry, tile laying, plumbing, and carpet installation. For the first time since my initial days at Wendy's, people truly depended on me. Being so productive put me in a strong frame of mind and helped me keep my nose clean.

My obsession with shortcuts and a life of crime had finally lifted completely off me. It was as if I'd been in the dark for the longest time, and now there was nothing but bright light all around me. My spirits were absolutely soaring.

Getting and maintaining that job was a turning point in

my life. Not only were Lash and Bruce proud of me, but more importantly I was proud of myself and it showed. Although my take-home pay of two hundred fifty dollars a week might not sound like much, I still had the huge benefit of the complimentary apartment. Having a free roof over my head made my money go far, and I lived very comfortably.

Aside from getting me out of Billie's, having my own place meant I had a potential home for Brandon.

When the social worker saw my bank statement with a figure in the thousands and read the letter of employment also detailing my free housing, she too was proud of me. "Mr. Huffman, I have to say I'm impressed by your consistent efforts to bring Brandon back into your life and put him in a proper home. Not many follow through with this process."

She went on to explain that although the plan was in motion, there were many steps involved on the road to custody. I would have a time of monthly visits with Brandon while the legalities were tended to in court. This period would also help reintroduce us and allow us to bond, preparing us for life together the way it should have been from the start.

At times, I was frustrated while waiting to get Brandon back, but I knew being put through the wringer was a standard part of the procedure. It was my proving ground. There was no reason to question or doubt anything in the process.

However, waiting wore my patience thin. I just wanted my

own flesh and blood where he belonged. I had to be content with our regular visits at the Houston Department of Health and Human Services.

The first time we reunited was in early 1989. He had turned five just a few months before in December, and now my twenty-fourth birthday was coming up. When Brandon came walking into the room, he lit up. My son instantly recognized me as his father.

I walked over, knelt down, reached for his hand, and gave him a little hug. I don't think I let his hand go till the end of that first visit. The two of us hung out and had a great time being father and son, carrying on conversations. He told me his adventures of meeting nice people, and I told him stories of my own childhood. I made a point to constantly reassure Brandon that he would soon come home with me. After the uncertainty and confusion the poor boy had gone through, I made it my undying mission to put his fears to bed.

Finally, about a year after I first talked with CPS, it happened. The court found me well suited to take custody of my son. Just like that, we were walking out into our new life together. I knew it was not going to be easy stepping into this new role and I had a lot of missed time to make up for, but it was a welcome challenge.

We got in the car I had borrowed from Lash and headed home. As we hopped on US 59 SW and headed out of downtown Houston, I felt overwhelmingly relieved to look down to my right to see Brandon holding his little suitcase on his lap and watching the skyline go by. It almost reminded me of my bus trip home from Pack 2. My son was free, as he deserved, and going home after such a long, unnecessary journey.

Now Brandon, my new dog Rocky 2, and I were under the same roof as a tight little Huffman family.

Now the nerves started setting in as I wondered what kind of dad I would be. *Great. I've got him,* I thought, *but now what do I do?* I was flying by the seat of my pants, basically figuring out the whole thing as I went.

I was also very sensitive to the trials Brandon had gone through with his mother. I had no doubt he had some issues over Angela's abandonment that had yet to reveal themselves. I'd learned she'd made some poor life choices, and she must have been in a really bad way to have handed him over to social services. I couldn't determine the extent of what he had seen, and I didn't bring it up. He was too young for the conversation, and I knew when the time was right, he would invite the discussion.

One thing I did right away was to enroll Brandon at the local elementary school. It was then that some of his struggles began to surface. According to the teacher, he was distracted a lot, didn't pay much attention, and seemed to be a little uncomfortable around other kids. Had it been today, maybe Brandon would have been diagnosed with attention deficit disorder or something. I don't know. But I made sure to get him a lot of tutoring to help him along so he would not fall behind as I once had.

I saw so much of myself in my son that I couldn't help but be a little overprotective. I had to make sure he received the guidance taken from me too early. As long as I was around, I would do everything it took to keep him on the right track.

11

EVERYTHING IN ITS PLACE

Another year passed, and life had settled into a nice pace. Brandon was a little more self-sufficient. We were in a nice little groove. My boss, Bruce, saw how hard I was working at the apartment complex and took a real shine to me. He decided to transfer me to a better job.

I started working at a warehouse facility Bruce owned called American Mini Storage on West 34th Street in Houston. Customers came there to buy packing supplies and rent self-storage units, U-Haul trucks, and trailers. The facility was not far from the apartment complex, but I had longer hours and wasn't able to simply walk home and check on my son anymore. I worked from seven in the morning till seven at night, so Brandon spent considerably more time at home without me. Brandon rose to the occasion like a responsible little man and had Rocky 2, the great protector, at his side the moment he walked in the door from school.

When I arrived home, we always had some dinner together

and asked each other about our days. Being the bachelor, I didn't put much thought into cooking. Still having a little Pack 2 rattling around in my head, I quickly exposed Brandon to the art of making spreads. He would watch in wonder as I took microwaved Ramen noodles, added chicken and cheese, and then crumbled crackers into the mix. The first time he took a bite of his dad's spread, his eyes lit up and he wolfed it down. He was definitely his father's son, and I got such a kick out of his enjoyment of these meals.

Other regular menu items at the Huffman residence were Hamburger Helper, cans of Hormel Chili and Dinty Moore beef stew, and plenty of Kraft Macaroni & Cheese, all perfect spread ingredients.

We had so much fun eating together and just hanging out laughing. There were moments I felt much more like Brandon's best friend or older brother than his dad. But as tight as our bond was, I still had to step outside of our casual relationship and discipline him when it was necessary.

Going on three years since Brandon came back into my life, my parole was finally at an end. The officer in charge offered sincere congratulations to me for having paid my debt to society in full, landing solidly back on my feet with a job and a home, and gaining custody of Brandon as well. The whole ordeal was totally over, and I was now just a regular law-abiding citizen with nothing to fear and no reason to look over my shoulder. Big Brother was history.

It was beyond satisfying to simply be working hard and providing for my boy. It was like that saying, "A place for everything and everything in its place." I had found a perfect fit in life.

During this time I bought my first car, a 1979 Ford Thunderbird. It was nothing special. Yeah, it was old and the paint was faded, but after Lash checked it out mechanically and gave it the thumbs-up, that T-Bird was all mine for fifteen hundred dollars. That car was all I needed to get from point A to point B and finally give the bus the big middle finger. Now there was no schedule to chase after like a dog, and I could take Brandon to school and go to work, the gym, and the grocery store on my own time.

It was great for my son and me and way overdue. This was what both of us had deserved since day one, and it was better to have it a little late than never.

My job at American Mini Storage was working out very well. Lash had shared his philosophy with me: "No matter what you do, make sure it's done to the best of your ability." I kept that ideal clear in my mind in my new role.

After putting in a relatively short amount of time, I had a handle on everything and was proud of my job. Instead of doing manual labor as I had at Wendy's, Pack 2, and the apartments, now I was relying on my mind, people skills, and computer skills. I worked in the air-conditioned office filling out contracts and helping customers with all their basic needs. There were only two of us working at American, covering twelve-hour shifts each.

Even though the days were long, it was worth every minute.

Then a little side job was offered to me. For whatever reason, even though Lash was not working security at Pier Club, he took it upon himself to moonlight on his own as a vigilante enforcer on the grounds late at night. He and his big friend Tony Norris, future WWF Superstar Ahmed Johnson, strolled around at night with their eyes peeled, just hoping to find strange things afoot so they could spring into action like superheroes. Lash asked me if I would think about coming along. When I considered all the help he had given me, of course I said yes. It was not one of my greatest decisions.

A week or so later, Lash came banging on my door at about one in the morning. "Junior," he said, huffing and puffing, "Tony and I have been watching these suspicious dudes for a while, and we know they're running a drug operation on the premises. We're gonna bust it up. Come on!"

I thought they were out of their minds, but I agreed anyway and got dressed. Outside, Lash and Tony were waiting.

My brother was right in my face, gassed up with excitement. "Are you ready, man?"

Still rubbing my eyes, I answered with slightly less enthusiasm. "I guess. What is it exactly you're doing again?"

Lash explained that he had been watching the comings and goings of these guys living in one of the apartments. He was convinced there was a drug operation going on, and he and Tony wanted to bust it up and turn the dudes over to the cops. For whatever reason, apparently my brother had a huge vendetta against drug dealers and made it his mission to seek them out whenever possible and wreck their operations.

I shrugged. "Whatever. Let's do this."

Then he reached into his bag and handed me an UZI. I swear to God my own brother, who was fully aware of everything I had been through with the streets, Wendy's, and prison, handed me a fully automatic gun straight out of a Rambo movie. For a split second, I looked around in the bushes for hidden cameras, expecting Allen Funt from *Candid Camera* to come busting out to reveal that it was all a gag.

"Jesus Christ! What the fuck do you want me to do with this thing, man?" I still could not believe Lash, the same guy who always preached about doing the right thing and working hard, was now pushing for me to invade some apartment with him as if we were the damn police.

I finally learned some local cops had encouraged Lash and Tony to do this kind of crap. The two of them had been responsible for many busts, allowing those policemen to get all the credit at the station. Man, they probably made detective rank for the work Tony and my brother had put in. But handing me this gun indicated they were getting a little power drunk.

"You stay right here while Tony and I run in. Anyone comes around this corner, you do what you have to, okay?"

There I was, a recently released ex-con busted for armed robbery, standing on a dimly lit sidewalk after one in the morning, holding an automatic firearm. If ever I had a true *What the fuck am I doing?* moment in my life, this was it.

While I tried to wrap my mind around the situation, Tony and Lash went smashing through somebody's front door like madmen, screaming at the top of their lungs, "Freeze!"

I was startled pretty good by the whole scene and was having Wendy's Bandits flashbacks. Even with the cops in on this deal, I still did not understand why my brother had me out here risking my life and freedom for the sake of his ego.

All of a sudden, a guy ran from behind the apartment and kicked open the gate heading my way.

Adrenaline kicked my senses into overdrive. I started shaking, the UZI teetering. I was terrified but somehow managed to utter a pretty unconvincing, "Hey, man, freeze," almost with a "please?"

It was a huge bluff just like the one I had used on Vernon in Pack 2, but in this case the stakes were higher.

After seeing the gun, the guy stopped dead in his tracks and immediately cowered. "What, man? What do you want me to do?"

I was still in shock and paranoid as hell that he might have a gun of his own.

Fortunately, he had nothing.

"Turn around and keep walking," I said and marched him to Lash and Tony.

They could not believe what I had for them.

Lash was beside himself. "Holy shit, Junior. Look what you got."

I just wanted to get out of there as fast as possible and put this nightmare back to bed.

While they rejoiced and added my catch to the peanut gallery of handcuffed and jail-bound fools, I gave Lash the gun. I was about to make a quick exit when out of nowhere my brother punched one of the cuffed guys in the stomach as hard as he could with a sickening thud.

The guy fell over and curled into a fetal position, coughing and gurgling.

That was it for me. It was not just Lash's display of brutality but the idea that one of those dudes might get out and come looking for payback. I knew I'd have more than one sleepless night thinking about it. It was totally unsettling and made my skin crawl.

After somehow managing a little sleep that night, I woke up at daybreak, thankful to resume a more conventional role at American Mini Storage. I thought I could rest easy for a while, but I was wrong.

As it happened, this attractive black woman came in to rent a storage unit. It was obvious she had just been crying. I stayed professional and minded my own business while trying to help her with the paperwork. When I led her out to the unit, she inspected the space quickly.

"I'll be right back with my stuff," she said.

I returned to the office to follow up on some other things. Within minutes, a commotion was coming from outside. The girl faced some black dude, presumably her ex-boyfriend, who was yelling at her.

I tried to remain calm, collected, and courteous. "Excuse me, but if you don't have a storage unit here or any other business you need assistance with, you'll have to leave. This is private property, and I can't have this here." I made a little motion to suggest he escort himself out of there.

The guy did not even make eye contact as he shoved me. "Man, get the fuck out of my face. This ain't any of your goddamn business." Then out of nowhere, he took a swing at me.

I saw it coming and moved my head back just in time to avoid an arching fist to the jaw. I just rolled my eyes and thought, *Oh boy, here we go*. I saw red and reacted. I took the guy down with a trip and a two-handed push slam, then bounced his head off the pavement like a basketball a couple of times.

I had to tell myself to stop or it might have gone too far, and it was enough as it was. I even had the wherewithal to go inside and call the cops on him because he could have had a gun in the car or something.

Making a proactive decision like that not only protected me physically but neutralized his chances of trying to call them first and claim I had attacked him out of nowhere.

When the police arrived, I recognized them as the guys from my old security job at the apartments. They took both sides of the story, and when they asked the girl for a third perspective, she told them I was a Good Samaritan who had come to her rescue.

The cops smiled and pulled me aside to congratulate me for my good work. They arrested that guy for assault even after he had taken a good ass-kicking. Not only that, but the girl gave me her number, telling me I should call sometime.

It was a validating scenario that added a little more swagger to my step. I was finally on the right side of the law. The invisible bonds I had felt for the last three years since being paroled from Pack 2 were broken for good.

I probably would have settled in for a life of contentment with my job at American. It was easy to envision working up the ladder, getting set up with a management position, and kicking back in my role. It was not the most thrilling and fulfilling thing to imagine doing, though, and I did daydream all the time of finding a little excitement.

Wouldn't you know it? Lash approached me one day, a determined look on his face, and said, "Let's start rasslin'."

It was surprising as hell, to say the least. "What do you mean?"

He tapped my chest. "Man, we've been fans for so long, and we both need something more in our lives. We both have size, we're athletic, and we've got personality off the fuckin' charts."

I stared, rubbing my chin. "How do we do it?"

"Brother, I've already got it all planned out. I found this school that'll teach us everything and even set us up in matches and shit. I'm telling you, Junior, we can do this. And we can make it."

Man, Lash was dead serious, and I was excited to go to this

place, get into the ring, and see what it was all about. I mean, seriously, what did we have to lose?

I asked Lash all kinds of questions about the training school, and he told me the place was run by the famous wrestler "Polish Power" Ivan Putski. Putski was a legend, especially with WWF back in the day. Apparently not long after I had been released from prison, Lash had run into Ivan, who had invited him to check out the facility. The idea had been in Lash's mind ever since.

The only other detail I needed to know was the cost.

"Man, it's not that much. It's only three thousand dollars for the eight-week class."

Three thousand? Man, it might as well have been three million. Although I did have five hundred saved up that could go toward the fee, I had no idea where the rest would come from. Lash told me that if I could put about half down, Putski would let a guy finance the rest in monthly installments. Still, I wondered how I would come up with that additional thousand.

A couple of days later, I was at American working as usual when Bruce walked in. We got to talking, and when I mentioned the wrestling school, he lit right up.

"Booker, that sounds like a great idea. I could see you going all the way. There's no doubt about it." Bruce told me he was a big wrestling fan, which I hadn't had a clue about. He wanted to hear more.

I explained how Lash had met Ivan Putski a few years back and told him all about it. Then I got to the part about my financial dilemma.

"How much more do you need?" he said. "A thousand? That's nothing. Tell you what. You've been doing such a great job for me, maybe it's about time for a bonus. What do you think?"

I didn't know what to say, but a smile came over my face. "Umm. A bonus?"

"Yeah, I was thinking around a thousand-dollar bonus so you can go to that school. Just go and do me proud, okay? What do you think?"

It was unbelievable. I shook his hand. "Deal."

Then I called Lash to tell him the good news.

After Bruce left the office, I sat in awe of his selflessness. He truly was a great guy with a golden heart along with a bank account large enough to assist in changing people's lives if and when he saw fit. I did not know why he had chosen me, especially with my criminal background, but I was sure glad he had.

With the fifteen hundred dollars in my pocket, I went with Lash down to South Dairy Ashford Street, where the school was located. When we pulled up to the building, the place was not at all what we'd expected. Instead of being some run-down dump in the basement of a church or some crummy warehouse with a beat-up ring and a leaky ceiling, Putski's wrestling school was a polished facility.

The school, known as Western Wrestling Alliance (WWA), was one of the most advanced operations you could imagine. It was like stepping into an actual WWF pay-per-view or something.

There were two brand-new rings, a weight room area, practice mats, and TV cameras covering all angles so we could even watch our matches. It was so professional it felt like we had already made it in the wrestling business the second we walked in.

It was evident that a lot of investor money had been solicited to make the WWA concept a reality and that there was more behind it than just a wrestling school. During the late sixties through the eighties, a promoter named Paul Boesch was responsible for the hugely popular *Houston Wrestling* television show on local KHTV channel 39. We had grown up watching it, but the promotion had faded away. Boesch, like so many other regional promoters, was forced to fold after the WWF and WCW dominated the scene with national TV and big-money contracts for all the best wrestlers in the country. Now, Ivan Putski and his investors felt they could capitalize on the void in Houston with the WWA. They helped finance the project by charging the very wrestlers in training they would feature at their shows.

The wrestling school program itself ran five days per week for eight weeks. About twenty of us were in the class. We were told that at the conclusion of our eight weeks, we'd be featured on *Houston Wrestling.* This was the real deal, and the whole thing was a little intimidating.

Wow. TV? I thought.

Lash looked at me, his eyebrows raised.

When we all got in the ring, one thing was evident: we were green as grass. Seriously, nobody knew a thing. It didn't help to discover that Ivan Putski himself was virtually useless as a trainer. We had watched the big star a few years back on TV wrestling for the WWF. We had never really noticed his lack of actual wrestling ability. Now we realized he'd just been an in-ring gimmick wrestler with a phenomenal physique.

Fortunately for me, where Putski fell short, one of the other trainers had some great things to offer as a coach. "Cowboy" Scott Casey had been a wrestler for the WWF just a few years earlier in the late eighties and had worked with guys like The Iron Sheik, Greg "The Hammer" Valentine, and Honky Tonk Man.

Scott took a liking to me and took me under his wing, making sure I understood the core fundamentals. From basic moves to the language wrestlers used with one another, he broke it all down and shared it with me.

Scott was also the one who encouraged my accidental breakthrough with my first character gimmick. At American Mini Storage one day, I was cleaning out an old storage locker someone had stopped making payments on and discovered a green army baseball cap. I thought it looked cool, so I put it on and made my way to the gym for a workout.

When Scott saw me, he called me over. "You've got to start wearing that hat all the time," he said. "From now on, this is going to be your character. You'll be G.I. Bro, America's greatest hero." He had a big smile on his face.

G.I. Bro? I thought. *What the fuck are you talking about?* But then I laughed. "Sure. Why not?" After all, this was professional wrestling, and some of the most famous guys had a great gimmick to connect with the crowd. G.I. Bro it would be.

At that time, the Gulf War had officially begun, and the country was charged with patriotism. It was crazy to have found that army cap during our nation's entry into a fierce conflict with Saddam Hussein and Iraq. If ever there was a prime example of being in the right place at the right time, it was when I cleaned out that storage unit in January of 1991.

To bring the G.I. Bro gimmick to life, I practiced with Cowboy Casey night in and night out. Most importantly, I was perfecting my technical in-ring work. It all came to me organically as if an instinctive part of me was emerging and taking over. All the time I had spent watching those kung fu movies as well as dancing with The Remote Controls suddenly came together. I used a lot of kick variations and chops with a dramatic Bruce Lee expression for effect, and the agility from those synchronized dance moves brought a fluidity to my style that made the routine believable.

While he watched my combinations, Cowboy laughed and shook his head. "Kid, you've got it. You're a natural."

BUILDING LASTING CHARACTER

As I developed the G.I. Bro character, I made a strategy to replace the legendary WWF Superstar Sgt. Slaughter, who had used an American hero gimmick to great effect for twenty-plus years in every wrestling organization in the country. At one point during the eighties, Slaughter was a character in the popular *G.I. Joe* cartoon and comic book series. He had even been made an action figure. He was a huge star. By this time, though, the Sarge was nearing the end of his career and playing an Iraqi sympathizer in one last run with Hulk Hogan.

At night I dreamed of replacing Slaughter and filling that Americana void. In the ring, nothing sold more than patriotism and great performances. I was developing both. Only time would tell.

During those eight weeks of training and at our first small shows, Cowboy Casey went to great lengths to assist with production value in my presentation. Soon I had not only a full set of army fatigues and combat boots but a huge American flag, which I carried and waved on the way to the ring. I also had an entrance song: "Soul Army" by Cameo.

When we did shows in local high school gyms, it was all about the presentation. Man, when my song hit, the whole place jumped up, even though I was a complete nobody. We had managed to tap directly into that patriotic vein just as planned, and it was really cool. I had a huge banner that said G.I. Bro: America's Greatest Hero. The kids rushed and jumped all over me as I came out holding a big red, white, and blue flag. I felt like a real-life superhero, and I loved it. No other feeling could compare to getting a reaction like that.

Having been nothing but a street kid my whole life, I'd never experienced this level of energy from a crowd before. It was even stronger than the feeling I'd gotten from those school talent shows when my group had something unique and everyone knew it, teachers included. I couldn't get enough. It was beyond adrenaline. After years of searching, I had finally found my niche. Who would have thought it would be in professional wrestling?

Suddenly I had a new outlet to express myself aside from my roles as Brandon's dad and American Mini Storage sales associate. It was a real kick to get off work in the evenings and head to the school. Every weeknight, I climbed out of my daytime norm and escaped into my alter ego as G.I. Bro. It was almost like being a kid and reliving carefree times again.

Having Lash there made it that much better. There we were, two Huffman brothers relearning how to play, only on a bigger stage.

Between work and wrestling, my hours were so long that I reached out for help with Brandon. My sister Carolyn, who had cleaned herself up, had invited Brandon to live with her. I was with him there several times a week and was so happy to see him with a solid roof over his head and food to eat. He was even doing better in school. I was making decent money, and the bills were paid. I felt like I was on my feet to stay.

I enjoyed meeting other wrestlers at our local shows and the camaraderie wherever we went, but I'll never forget when we reached the end of the eight weeks for the WWA training camp and the big names arrived. We were about to perform for our first TV show, and it would be in front of a live audience of a few thousand people. We would also be competing with more established names in the business who were brought in to give credibility to the WWA product.

By this point, all of us had reservations about the level of teaching and insight we had received from Ivan Putski. We felt burned. Had it not been for the good graces of the Cowboy, I may have bailed on professional wrestling altogether.

That night I ran to see the match listing posted on the wall. I would face Dusty Wolfe, who had been a well-known jobber for the WWF since the mideighties under various names, including Dale Wolfe. He had never won a match. It was his sole position to lose and make the stars look fantastic. Every successful WWF wrestler during the eighties had no doubt beat Dusty to a pulp on many occasions. That was just how it went for some guys, but it was a paycheck and TV time.

Dusty had amassed his own level of recognition and had a ton of experience in the ring. Nerves aside, I was very curious what he would say as we went over our match backstage. Although guys like Dusty were paid by the WWF to lose without getting much offense in during matches, they were usually the main event when they hit the independents like WWA.

I was smart enough to know Dusty Wolfe was smarter than me. His experience was like a set of encyclopedias. He had all my respect from the moment he gave me the classic gentleman's handshake, which is one of those unspoken rules in wrestling. Simply put, you very gently shake another wrestler's hand out of respect. Ric Flair is the master of this tradition, which was around long before my time. Pitifully ignorant is the performer who comes in with a kung fu grip, trying to exert his strength. He will find himself and his belongings rammed into a Dumpster faster than the speed of light.

As it got close to match time, I was anxious and looking to Dusty to take me by the hand and explain what to expect. He had been through it all, and I needed reassurance and guidance.

Dusty was great about it. He was a personable and professional dude, and we had a great match. I got the one-two-three pin, and the crowd was hot from beginning to end. I had a hard time containing myself and could not keep the grin off my face as I walked to the back, high-fiving all the fans along the way.

When Dusty and I walked through the curtain, I expected

everyone to congratulate me.

Instead, I was shocked to see Ivan standing there fuming. "You piece of shit," he said in front of everyone back there. "That's one of the worst fucking things I ever saw in all my years. What a joke. You didn't do anything I taught you, and what you did was horrible. Why bother wasting your time and mine?"

I was completely taken aback and did not say anything. Dusty, the fans, and I had thought the match was solid, but I would be lying if I said he didn't shake my confidence. I began questioning myself. Why was I trying to pull this wrestling thing off?

Just then a godsend came my way. Joe Blanchard, the legendary old-school pro wrestling promoter and the father of The Four Horsemen and Brain Busters member Tully Blanchard, approached. "That was one of the greatest matches I ever saw for someone so green in the business. Wow!"

I couldn't believe it. It was rejuvenating to have one of the most respected men in the history of professional wrestling give me a moment of his time. I concluded that Ivan Putski was just a putz.

After my match with Dusty, things took off and we did more WWA shows. As our matches played and I saw myself right there on the television, it sank in. *That's me. G.I. Bro.*

Houston was a relatively small market, and people began recognizing me everywhere I went. It was humbling and even sometimes embarrassing when I would be working at American Mini Storage and a customer's little son would ask for an autograph.

Bruce, always my biggest fan, got a huge kick out of it. "See, Booker," he would say with a smile, "I told you!"

The WWA shows were getting bigger by the week. I was also meeting more established, internationally recognized performers on a regular basis. This was a crucial aspect of learning the business. Just as Joe Blanchard had encouraged me, other guys also generously offered their time and perspectives.

One night in late 1991, another big WWA show was being taped for *Houston Wrestling*. It was in an arena downtown known as The Summit, a famous venue that had hosted everything from WWF and WCW shows to some of the biggest acts in music over the years, including Paul McCartney, Aerosmith, Genesis, and Prince. Many well-known wrestlers like Ox Baker, Manny Fernandez, Jose Lothario, Black Bart, and Sam Houston, all Texas favorites, were brought in just for the event. There was a lot of promotion and excitement building up to our show.

I pulled in to the back building's talent entrance in my piece-of-crap 1979 Ford T-Bird.

A security guard walked up to me, cracking half a smile. "Can I help you?"

I could tell he was staring my car up and down, and what a sight it was. It had this laughable, sunbaked paint job peeling off in sections, completely bald tires, and a wire coat hanger sticking out of the hood as my antenna.

"Yeah, man, I'm one of the wrestlers for tonight's show." I

pointed at my gear bag, which was sitting on a seat bursting at the seams with hideous orange foam.

"Oh, okay. Just pull straight ahead and find any open spot."

Any self-esteem I'd had was destroyed. As I walked into the building, I laughed it off but came to a serious conclusion. As soon as I got out of there, I was buying a new car.

As I stood backstage preparing, seven thousand fans stomped, rocking the rafters overhead. I was extremely nervous to walk out in front of them. The whole place rattled as if an earthquake had struck. Then I heard a different sound that shook me even more.

"We want Bro! We want Bro!"

The crowd was chanting for me! Losing my mind, I began to pace as my stomach twisted itself into knots.

Cowboy Casey walked back and saw my restlessness. "How you feeling? A little nervous, brother?" He had a huge, obnoxious grin on his face, and I hated him for it.

"Nah, I'm cool, man. Ready to go."

Cowboy raised his eyebrows, clearly not believing a word I said. "Good! Because you're on next."

Ah, man!

Well, suffice it to say, the match went extremely well. Even that early on, I had a work style that was easy to manage and cohesive with any opponent's as long as he had the slightest athletic ability and decent reflexes. I was so anxious that night that I don't even remember who I wrestled. It seemed like it was over as soon as it had begun, even though it was a scheduled ten-minute match—an eternity inside the ring.

What's most memorable about that night is Ox Baker. Ox was about as famous as a guy could get in professional wrestling. He had been performing all over the world since 1962 and was instantly recognized wherever he went with his pointed eyebrows, giant Fu Manchu mustache, and bald head.

I was sitting on a bench unlacing my boots when the massive Ox sat down beside me. "Kid, I saw you out there. I've been around a long time and I'm telling you, with your athleticism, poise, and that crowd reaction, you've got something special. You have the ability to make it as far as you want to take it."

I just looked at him, speechless and overwhelmed.

He advised me to expect racism to surface everywhere, from other wrestlers and up to the office. "They'll try to hold you down if they can, out of nothing but jealousy and feeling threatened. I've seen it time and time again. The key is to just deal with it, and eventually no one can mess with you because you'll have made it. When someone draws and makes money, all the bullshit goes away."

I was grateful for the wise insight but thought, *Why is he telling me this? Is there an agenda behind all this?*

There wasn't. He was just a guy who had seen it all during his thirty years in professional wrestling and enjoyed giving something back. I'm glad he did. I would remember Ox's advice forever.

As my wrestling education continued, I was not the only one finding success. Lash had also been excelling as one of the best big men climbing the ranks in our local independent scene with the WWA. He picked up on the training as quickly as I did and was really enjoying pursuing his lifelong dream.

One thing we agreed about early on was to keep separate and not let the fact that we were brothers be a reason to team up. We even kept our brotherhood from the public so that when we were billed to wrestle each other, which we often were, the people thought we were just two random wrestlers going at it. Our matches usually stole the show due to our years of chemistry and the fact that we had both swiped every cool move we could from WWF shows on TV.

Being adversaries was fun, and it was just like wrestling around when we were kids, but one time our kayfabe rivalry was responsible for one of the most entertaining reactions we ever got. It happened one night in Galveston at the Moody Civic Center when Carolyn, Gayle, Billie Jean, and even Bonita showed up to see what their brothers had been up to. Brandon was even there to see his dad and uncle in action.

Back then, Lash had this great heel gimmick as Super Collider the Atom Smasher and had a tag team partner, a former NFL player for the Houston Oilers named Avon Riley. That night Lash and I wrestled each other. After having been down and out for a few minutes, I was mounting a comeback and getting the upper hand. Just as I was really starting to pour it on with punches, chops, and kicks, Riley ran up the aisle, slid in the ring, and began beating me down. Lash jumped in, and they both convincingly put the boots to me. It was a classic two-on-one confrontation. The crowd was booing and throwing all kinds of things into the ring. That's when Gayle jumped in.

Wait. Gayle? Yes, indeed.

My sister Gayle did not realize everything she was watching was just a show, and after losing her mind, she ran down into the ring to intervene. She went ballistic, thinking Lash and some stranger were pummeling her little brother. You had to see it.

Security stepped in and was about to haul her off, but we pulled them aside and told them the situation. In all honesty, it made the whole thing that much more believable. The fans ate it all up. As you can imagine, we laughed about that in the locker room for weeks.

During this time, I knew a breakthrough was on the horizon. Sure, I was still making only a hundred bucks a night, but I could feel the potential energy surging all around. I had never thought professional wrestling would be my ticket to an extraordinary life. At best, in the beginning I had seen it as an amusing side project, but slowly and surely the relatively minor doses of local fame and our small payoff envelopes convinced me to invest myself for as long as it would take.

Well, as I had promised myself earlier, the time was finally at hand to buy a new car. The T-Bird was finished, so I went down to PC Motors and found a black and gold 1986 Chevrolet Camaro IROC Z. That Z had the image I was trying to project in my career. It was all muscle and sounded intimidating roaring down the road with the windows down and the stereo volume up to full blast.

My cruising, however, came to an abrupt stop days later. I was driving home from the gym when a woman made a left turn through a red light and T-boned me directly on my driver's side just behind the door. I could not believe it. My new Z was pulverized.

While we waited for the cops, I learned that the lady had just been fired from her job and had been crying her eyes out when she'd run the red. I tried to comfort her and took a better look at the damage. It became instantly apparent how badly hurt I would have been if she had hit me just about a foot closer to the front. The frame would have completely caved in on me.

In the end, it all worked for the best. I used the insurance payoff to restore the Z with rims, fresh blue paint, and a custom stereo system. No matter where I went for years after, everyone knew Booker T was coming.

There would be yet another memorable incident with the Camaro. This gorgeous Hispanic girl named Delia LeBaron came into American Mini Storage one day. I found out she was an exotic dancer from this joint called Rick's, and we just hit it off and started seeing each other over the course of a few months.

Her place was only five minutes away from my mine, which allowed us to spend a lot of time together. She even had a young son named Tyler, who was around six or seven and got along famously with Brandon when I brought him over. It was not long before we took things to the next level and I moved into her apartment.

I reveled in my relationship with Delia for far more reasons than the fact that she was a sexy, uninhibited girl. Among black guys back then, there was a well-known code that said you should have a devoted stripper girlfriend to fall back on for financial support if times got tough. Well, I had mine! Sure, it boosted my ego. Hell, yeah, it was a self-indulgent philosophy. But man, I felt like I had everything under control.

Then it all came crashing down around me. At about two in the morning on a Saturday, I was sound asleep, resting up for the long drive to a WWA show in Dallas. All of a sudden, I was startled awake.

"Booker, wake up!" Delia had just come back from work and was frantically shaking my shoulders.

Still groggy and now a little annoyed, I looked at her. "What's going on?"

She seemed wired and a little out of it. I wondered if she was on some kind of drug. "Delia, if you don't stop this bullshit so I can go back to bed, I'm gettin' the fuck out of here and going someplace I can."

She didn't like that.

I started packing up my gear while she pleaded with me to stay, but it was too late. My mind was made up.

She continued stammering nonsense as I walked out the door.

After walking down the stairs to the ground floor, I tossed my bags into the Z and hopped in. No sooner had I reached to start the ignition than I heard an unmistakable sound.

Gunfire.

I looked up, and there was Delia out on the second-floor balcony shooting off rounds at me with a .45. I panicked, ducked, and somehow managed to start the car and peel out of there. My adrenaline was rushing, and my hands were shaking out of control. It was like an out-of-body experience to be that close to death—even closer than I'd come to that bus stop stabbing.

I pulled over to a gas station to process what had just happened and to make sure I hadn't been hit. After realizing I was okay, I got out of the Camaro to find that the hood and passenger door were full of bullet holes. *Jesus Christ,* I thought, *that was too close.*

After calling the cops, I waited, trying to catch my breath and count my blessings.

To my surprise, when the police showed up, they put me in cuffs and were about to arrest me. Apparently Delia had also called them, claiming I was the one with the gun and this was all my fault.

Fortunately, after I explained the truth to them and pointed out the holes in the Z, they arrested Delia and put her in jail. I declined to press charges, and they let her out the next day.

Another couple of days later, while trying to put her and the incident out of my mind and far from my life, I found out Delia had shot herself in the chest and died. I could not wrap my mind around any of it. At one point I had really cared for Delia, and the tragedy haunted me for a long time.

It was only after Delia's suicide that I discovered her connection to Texan cult leader Ervil LeBaron, who was responsible for instigating twenty-five murders through his religious followers, quite similar to what Charles Manson had done in Los Angeles in 1969. In 1980 LeBaron was sentenced to life in prison, where another inmate murdered him in 1981. LeBaron had over thirteen wives and more than fifty children. As it happened, Delia was one of his daughters.

With that traumatic experience behind me, I focused on my wrestling career. After only a couple of months' worth of WWA shows, the money ran out and Putski was broke. He had spent way too much trying to bring in top-name talent, given family members undeserved jobs, and overextended the show production.

As a result, the company imploded. All the investors saw their pockets empty before their very eyes and were not happy. All our promised big shows vanished. We went from playing hot Texas venues packed with live-wire crowds to performing in the ghetto in these rat-filled warehouse dumps facilitated on shoestring budgets. I went from my usual hundred dollars a night to twenty-five. It was a morale killer for all the boys.

At one of our last WWA shows before the whole nightmare finally folded for good, Putski thought he could pit Lash and me against each other in real life. When he was with me, he called me the better of the two. Then he whispered in Lash's ear, "Booker's trying to fuck you over and leave you high, dry, and alone."

Just after that, Lash and I spoke and realized what Putski was trying to do. "Fuck this, Bro," I said. "That little punk is trying to ruin our relationship. I'm out of here."

I didn't need to be manipulated by a twerp like Putski. Having been in the business for a while now, I had met many other promoters. I had options. I grabbed my stuff, kicked the door open, and stormed out of the WWA. I never looked back.

13

NEVER LOOKING BACK

After my departure, Lash eventually left the WWA for good as well. Soon we met up with this cool cat named Tugboat Taylor, who was promoting a little shoestring organization called Texas All Pro Wrestling and wanted to give us an opportunity. I was interested, but after working for him a couple of times, I realized Tugboat had nothing and could pay nothing. The only reason we stayed on was for the chance to be active in the ring until we found something better.

We didn't care that we were wrestling in bingo halls, bowling alleys, and at car washes. It was fun. I just wanted to put my boots on, become G.I. Bro, and do my thing. It didn't matter if we drew only fifty people to the show at the Unicorn Ballroom on a Saturday night as long as it provided that all-important escape from the doldrums of the previous week at American Mini Storage.

For one particular event, though, Tugboat initiated a new method of ticket sales. He thought it might motivate the performers and possibly bring in more money for everyone across the board if we were responsible to sell our own tickets for a percentage of the take. I was given fifteen tickets to sell. With all of my friends in the area, I sold those tickets the first day. *Cool,* I thought, *that was easy money.*

My opponent that night in the main event was a guy named "Killer" Tim Brooks. He was a fellow Texan and was a twenty-year veteran who had wrestled in every major promotion. He had a huge reputation and was a notorious savage in the ring who pulled no punches, worked stiff as a board, and legitimately took every liberty he could against opponents. He was regarded as a loose cannon.

I kept my usual composure, but inside I was a mess and wondered how to go about handling him. Just a few minutes before we were set to go out, I stood there in my G.I. Bro fatigues with the American flag in hand.

When Brooks approached, he was very personable. Like a true pro, he went over some fine points and certain spots for the match. Aside from those, he just wanted to wing it. Brooks was an old-school type who liked to spontaneously call the matches while in the ring. I was excited to see that kind of style firsthand and learn from it. And man, did I ever learn.

When it was time to hit the ring, Brooks walked through the curtain first with all the charm and disposition of an escaped mental patient. He growled at the fans as he made his way to the ring, even charging them, drool flying from his giant beard in every direction.

As "Soul Army" blasted over the loud speakers, the small but raucous crowd screamed for me like an audience twice their size. I paraded to the ring with my flag flying high.

As soon as I walked through the ropes, Brooks kicked my ass. I mean, he was really kicking my ass! He was laying in with the stiffest kicks and punches I had ever felt outside of a real fight—and harder than most of those. I had no idea what to do. Brooks was not doing any of what we had discussed backstage just a few minutes prior. To put it mildly, I was shocked and more than a little worried.

Shit, I thought, *now I know why they call him Killer.*

Then without warning, he dumped me out of the ring onto my face. Maybe it was a bad idea to let him call the match on the fly. Probably. No, *definitely.*

As I tried to compose myself, Brooks pulled a two-by-four out from underneath the ring and started smashing me flat across the back with Babe Ruth swings.

I was at a complete loss. All I kept thinking was, *What do I do? Do I start fighting back? Is somebody from the back going to do something?*

Then finally after throwing me back in the ring, Brooks whispered, "Okay, kid, fight back. Get the comeback, and take it home for the win."

He started bumping for me all over the ring, putting on a professional performance like I had never seen before. In an instant, I rolled him up and got the pin. The place went berserk.

I stood in the corner for a few seconds, catching my breath and wondering what had just happened. The two of us had told a classic, old-fashioned story of good versus evil, with the hero prevailing in the end. It was perfect, however unpredictable it had been. There's no doubt it looked believable to the fans, because it was far closer to a murder scene than they realized, with "Killer" Tim Brooks leading the show.

After Brooks finished selling his injury, he got up and stormed toward the back and through the curtain. As I watched, I was still a little worried about what to expect.

I quickly rolled out of the ring and went straight to the dressing room, thinking, *Did I do something in the ring to piss him off?*

Much to my surprise, Brooks walked right up to me with a big smile and a handshake. "Kid, you're gonna be all right. You didn't panic, and I was testing you. You kept your composure and still went with the rest of the match as planned." He gave me a pat on the back and said to everyone in the room, "That's how you do it, boys."

I was speechless and so excited I had passed his test. Well, I *had* wanted a learning experience.

At the end of the night when it was time for our payoffs, things got really interesting. As agreed, "Killer" Tim got his fee of five hundred dollars. He shook my hand once more and went his way. I held out my hand and waited for Tugboat Taylor to dish out what I expected to be anywhere from seventy to a hundred dollars. He started counting my cash in one-dollar bills—one, two, three, four, five, six, seven, eight, nine, ten. He stopped.

I thought he was kidding, but after I had sold all those tickets for him, he was really giving me ten bucks. I was beyond mad and temporarily lost my mind. I took the ten dollar bills, wadded them up, and threw them in his face. "You son of a bitch, who in the fuck do you think you are? You're lucky I don't put you through that wall. I'll never work for you again, and I'll make sure everyone in the business knows what a piece of shit you are."

Tugboat stared and did not say a word.

I picked up my gear bag and walked out of there, leaving the money on the floor. I didn't care how much of a veteran he was or who he knew in the business. There was no question my talent was worth far more than that. Tugboat was lucky I hadn't felt like rearranging some teeth that night.

Though the experience with Tugboat left a sour taste in my mouth, it did not deter me from the goal of taking G.I. Bro all the way. Lash and I continued working smaller shows throughout Houston and concentrated on honing our craft until another opportunity presented itself.

Eventually we got booked into a show in Amarillo. We would make a hundred bucks working against a cowboy-themed tag team called the Young Guns. The drive from Houston to Amarillo is about six hours in clear weather. Of course, the Saturday morning we started driving we ran directly into an ice storm, and our road trip became a treacherous eighteen-hour ride in the Z. My Camaro had around 300 hp and was, of course, rear wheel drive. A car like that in those conditions was like a bicycle with flat tires on a frozen pond. We were all over the place, and I think we averaged twenty-five miles per hour at best.

On the way, we passed about three wrecks. One was so bad that the guy was trapped in his car in the ditch. When we pulled over to help, we saw he had a gruesome leg break. The sight made my stomach turn, and Lash and I tried to comfort the poor guy as much as possible.

Since no one else was around, we agreed to drive on and send help the second we came across a phone or a cop. A couple more miles down the highway, we spotted an officer, who took our report, called for an ambulance, and drove away toward the accident.

When we finally made it to the show we had a good match, but after eighteen hours in the Z the event seemed like an afterthought. Because of the storm and our exhaustion, the promoter was cool enough to let us sleep over at his place, which was great because that hundred-dollar envelope wouldn't have even covered a motel room and food, let alone a gas tank refill.

Our resolve to make it to the appearance that night instead of turning around and going home yielded us one of the richest payoffs we would ever receive in the business. It just so happened that "General" Skandor Akbar, a once-famous wrestler who was now an influential manager and talent scout, had seen us. Word got back to us in the locker room that we'd impressed Akbar and he was on his way to talk with us.

Lash and I started getting dressed, talking about the General during his days as a great heel manager on the Dallas-based *World Class Championship Wrestling* TV show in the mid-eighties. WCCW had gone bankrupt by 1990 and had been redeveloped as the Global Wrestling Federation (GWF), where Akbar was currently working.

When we were almost packed up, the man himself walked in. He politely introduced himself and got straight to the point. "Why don't you guys come work for me and do a couple shows down at the Sportatorium in Dallas?"

Was he serious? In less than twenty-four hours, I had gone from the counter at American Mini Storage to a death-defying ride through an ice storm to receiving an invitation from the legendary "General" Skandor Akbar to wrestle at the Sportatorium, the original home of WCCW.

I had only one question. "Where do we sign up?"

Akbar took our phone numbers and said he would be in touch with all the details.

That night in the darkness, Lash and I stayed up talking like kids at a slumber party. We were too busy planning our futures as rich and famous wrestlers to waste our time with mere sleep.

True to his word, Akbar soon gave Lash a call and invited him to Dallas to meet with GWF booker "Hot Stuff" Eddie Gilbert at the Sportatorium. Apparently, they were really impressed by

Lash's frame of six foot five and almost three hundred pounds and saw him as the priority on their list between the two of us.

Undaunted and wanting to see what it was all about, I was sure to be sitting shotgun when Lash started the 250-mile drive to Dallas. Although I had a feeling Lash was slightly annoyed that I was tagging along, there was no way I would miss out on the opportunity at hand.

"Come on, man," I said, "we're a package deal."

He shook his head and smiled. "Okay, Junior, we'll see."

When we walked into the Sportatorium, I was in awe. The place was old, rickety, and smelled like stale beer and popcorn. It had all the charm of a hundred-year-old Texas honky-tonk and was the site of thousands of historic matches and the launching pad for dozens of legendary wrestlers, such as Kerry Von Erich, Scott "Bam Bam" Bigelow, "Ravishing" Rick Rude, and a young Mark Calaway, who later gained famed as The Undertaker.

Akbar walked out and greeted us, then led us to a back office, where Eddie Gilbert sat at a desk. We introduced ourselves and sat down while Eddie started up a conversation with Lash.

Eddie kept glancing at me quizzically, then finally said, "Who's this guy? Is he a worker too?"

"Yes," Lash said.

"What's your name?"

When I told him I was Booker T, he lit right up. "Wait, what? I know who you are. You're the workers from Houston with the bad attitudes."

I looked at Lash and immediately realized what Eddie was talking about. Tugboat had been trying to blackball us, throwing the Huffman brothers under the bus and talking about us to everyone within earshot. We quickly explained the debacle of the ten-dollar payout, which made Akbar and Eddie burst out laughing.

"Yeah," the General said, "that's Tugboat all right."

Eddie said, "We've been looking for a clean-cut baby face team, and you guys fit the bill. We haven't had black wrestlers in the GWF yet, and I want to give you guys a chance to break some ground."

It sounded great to us.

Eddie rubbed his chin, trying to come up with gimmick names for us. He looked at Lash and said, "Stevie Ray. You're going to be Stevie Ray, in honor of my favorite blues guitarist, Stevie Ray Vaughan."

Then he looked at me. "Booker T? That's fucking great. I couldn't come up with a better name than that if I tried."

He went on to describe his vision for the team he called The Ebony Experience. We would come out wearing suits and sunglasses and be a take-no-shit duo that commanded respect with a confident, slick presentation.

What was there to say no to?

Akbar then told us we would make a hundred dollars each per appearance for five ESPN tapings and promos announcing our eventual arrivals.

Lash and I were over the top with excitement. We could not

believe how cool and genuine Eddie came off. He explained that the crowd at the Sportatorium would likely be extremely racist. They weren't used to big "uppity niggers" coming in and throwing their white boys around, but he said, "You watch—they'll side with you in time."

Akbar and Eddie congratulated us and told us to get ready for a bright future and that they had big plans for us already set in motion. It was far beyond anything Lash and I had expected.

Just before we left, we were told to be at the Sportatorium in two weeks with matching black suits and not to be late.

Lash and I ran out of there as if we'd just won the lottery and drove all the way to Houston on top of the world. Two weeks later, we were on the road to Dallas again with visions of finally making the big time.

As we walked in the back entrance, Akbar came up to us with a grave look on his face.

"Hey, General," Lash said. "Today's the day, huh? Where's Eddie? We want to go over our material and make sure everything's tight."

Akbar looked at the floor and then at us. "Eddie got fired, guys. He's no longer around, but I took his place and I'm going to take care of you as much as I can."

My heart sank. Eddie was the booker who had arranged all the matches and produced the promos—practically the entire show. I began to imagine everything falling apart and us driving home empty-handed.

To Akbar's credit, he immediately stepped up and said, "We don't know what Eddie had planned for you, but you're still getting your shot. We want to see what you guys can do as a team, okay?"

We thanked him and tried to calm ourselves while changing into our suits.

"Don't worry," Lash said. "We've got this. We're going to blow them away."

A short while later, Akbar came into the dressing room to tell us a little bit about our opponents for the night. "They're called Brute Force, and they're two big, thuggish white bruisers with bleached spiked hair, kind of like The Nasty Boys. They're a little sloppy in the ring, so be careful."

We were up for anything.

When our match was called, I looked at Lash and slapped him on the back. "Let's do this."

Then out we went. As ready as we thought we were, nothing could have prepared us for what happened next.

Lash and I walked through the curtain into the Sportatorium to a deafening chorus of racist jeers. "Fuck you, niggers. Get the fuck out of here."

Eddie had not been kidding. It felt as if we had traveled forty or fifty years back in time. Even little old ladies and children were right at the forefront taking part in the good old hillbilly hate-fest. It was unbelievable.

The match was all right but definitely not one of our best performances. The antics of the crowd affected me mentally far more than I had anticipated. My mind kept going blank while I dodged cups of tobacco spit and half-eaten corndogs.

Still, that event managed to produce one memory worth holding on to. One of the Brute Force guys was really giving me the business in a corner with elbows and kicks to the gut. When he went to whip me across the ring to the opposite corner, I reversed it midway and threw him into the turnbuckles instead. With a sudden burst, he instantly came charging back out and clotheslined me onto the mat. That's when it happened.

As soon as my head thumped against the canvas, something just clicked inside of me and without even thinking, I stuck my legs straight into the air and gave myself a little sideways push using my hands. Kicking around to the left, I quickly spun myself on my back in a full counterclockwise circle. The momentum and weight of my legs allowed me to slightly pull myself up and into a kneeling position. The move was basically a short breakdancing backspin I had done during routines with The Remote Controls. I'd only done it here and there during training sessions back in the WWA and didn't consider it to be anything special.

When it just sort of happened in the match, what struck me most was the smattering of applause and cheers I heard. I thought, *Did I really just get some respect for doing that? I'll be damned.* It was sparse, but I instantly heard it, mostly because it was about the only break in the deluge of racial slurs.

It was a small moment, one I am sure not many caught, but it made my confidence soar all the same. I knew from that point forward that if there was a time during a match when I needed to connect with the audience a little, this was an ace up my sleeve. It was a nice asset. The move, which announcer Mark Madden later dubbed the Spin-A-Roonie, would become one of my most recognized character trademarks.

Aside from the debut of the Spin-A-Roonie, our first match as The Ebony Experience by no means reinvented the wheel of tag team wrestling. The racist crowd had definitely thrown us a little off balance, and Brute Force was not exactly a stellar team to work with. However, overall, I thought we displayed enough athleticism and charisma to show the General how much potential we possessed.

I was right.

Akbar greeted us at the curtain. "You were fantastic. You have jobs here at the Sportatorium with GWF every Friday night. And don't worry about the crowd. They'll be on your side before you realize it."

It was the news Lash and I had been waiting to hear since day one at the WWA training school.

Now keep in mind, I was still very much employed by Bruce Gasarch at American Mini Storage. My schedule now was Sunday through Friday, when I still worked my usual twelve-hour shifts. On Fridays, Bruce would let me leave at around two in the afternoon to make the shows on time. Saturdays were really the only day I could see Brandon and catch up on my sleep.

Working at American was becoming even more amusing

since I had become somewhat of a local celebrity. My face was on the local playbills for upcoming shows, which Bruce happily plastered all over the front doors and inside the office. I could rest assured that even if one of the customers didn't make the connection between the face on the poster and the guy renting them a U-Haul, Bruce would quickly point it out.

"This is Booker T," he'd say, putting an arm around my shoulders. "He's going to be a big star."

I wanted to hide, but eventually I learned to go with it, flash smiles, and answer all the questions as entertainingly as possible.

By the summer of 1992, Lash and I had been wrestling almost three years and were enthralled by the power of entertaining people. In the months since our debut at the Sportatorium, the tide had turned in our favor. The once bigoted audience had gone from hating us to considering us their favorite team on the GWF roster, just as Akbar had said in the beginning. Not only had we won over the old fans, but we were drawing more and more people to the shows each week. What had begun as three hundred people soon multiplied to upwards of three thousand, due in part to the word on the street about this team called The Ebony Experience.

As Lash and I stood behind the curtain waiting for our music to hit and the lights to go down, all we could hear was a collective, "Ebony, Ebony . . ." It was pure magic.

Eventually we went on to win the GWF Tag Team Championships in front of our entire family during an ESPN taping.

It felt as if we had reached the pinnacle of the business. In some ways, we had. After just two years spent battling it out in the trenches of the independent scene, the two Huffman boys had made good. And yet we were just getting started.

I even had the opportunity to wrestle overseas. A GWF referee named James Beard thought my ring work and style were so unique that he took it upon himself to book me on brief tours of Japan and Korea. "They'll love you over there," he said. "You incorporate moves reminiscent of martial arts but with American street bravado. They'll eat it up."

Sometimes it was hard to process it all. Here was this ex-con traveling the world and making a name for himself in a business he had dreamed about as a kid. Things were escalating beyond my wildest expectations. I had magazine feature requests, public autograph appearances, and even television and newspaper interviews. The whole frenzy was worth its weight in gold in terms of exposure, increasing show attendance and of course bringing bigger paydays.

Then one night, just as Lash and I were about to head out to the ring, one of my biggest supporters and peers in the GWF, "Maniac" Mike Davis, came into the dressing room with huge news. "Hey, guys, I just got off the phone with Sid Vicious. He wants to know if you'd be interested in coming to Atlanta."

The needle scratched right off the record.

Sid Vicious was one of the biggest and baddest wrestlers to step over the top rope for companies like WCW and the WWF.

He had just finished a huge program with Hulk Hogan and then had a falling out with WWF President Vince McMahon and decided to make the transition into the booking position in the WCW front office. He was looking for new talent to propel the roster to the next level and he was interested in Lash and me, of all people. Mike gave us Sid's number.

Later that night, Lash picked up the phone and gave him a call.

I sat next to him the whole time, trying to listen in and dying to know what Sid was saying.

When Lash hung up, he was almost speechless. "Sid's trying to make a name for himself and impress the brass at WCW with his ability to spot fresh talent. He thinks we have what it takes to become big stars. He wants to know if we'd like to come work at WCW."

My heart skipped a beat.

"He told us to sit tight, keep working hard at GWF. He's going to get us over to Atlanta as soon as possible and make us his central focus."

Man, this was serious material to process.

Days of sitting with enthusiastic wonder eventually became weeks of nerve-wracking waiting. Just when it seemed we wouldn't get the call, the phone rang.

"I got you guys in. Are you ready for the opportunity to come down to Atlanta for your WCW tryout?"

We told Sid it was what we'd been waiting for our entire lives and we would see him soon.

Like little kids on the last day of school before summer break as the clock struck three, Lash and I jumped and hugged each other. The energy was in the air. We ran around and packed up everything we needed for a few weeks and tossed it into the back of my Camaro.

Then we called the General and Mike Davis to tell them the news, and they arranged an impromptu send-off party in the Sportatorium parking lot.

After everyone wished us well and said their good-byes, Lash and I sprinted to the Z, kicking up rocks and dust clouds as we jumped in. I cranked the engine over with a loud explosion of American muscle car exhaust and turned the radio up to full blast.

My foot smashed the pedal, and Lash and I peeled out in the arid Texas dirt. We skidded out onto the road that would take us all the way to Atlanta, where we would permanently alter our lives as we knew them. The windows were down, and the wind whipped in our laughing faces. And it was hot, boy. We could barely breathe in such relentless heat, the *Harlem Heat*.

But that story has yet to be told—and it's coming sooner than you think.

Now can you dig that?

ACKNOWLEDGMENTS

I would like to thank my parents, Booker T Sr. and Rosa Huffman, for inspiring me and instilling good values I could build on later in life; my sister Carolyn for providing key insight to my father's backstory; my wife, Sharmell, for devoting her time to read this story and assist in the editorial process; Medallion Media Group President Adam Mock for believing in the story of my life before I stepped into the ring; Bruce Gasarch for trusting me and keeping my head above water; Brenda Sullivan for peace of mind; and lastly, Andrew William Wright for his creative vision while piecing together the amazing story of my past.

—Booker T

I would like to thank my parents, John and Martha Wright, for their undying support; Adam Mock for the opportunity to write my second Medallion Press book; Emily Steele for her due diligence on this project; and Booker T for trusting me as a new friend and partner to write such an in-depth and personal journey into his past.

—Andrew William Wright